Susan —
To God's a[d]...
for your life!
May the Lord bless
& inspire your life.
Enjoy!

don't blink

John M[...]

Praise for

don't blink

"A lot of people spend their whole life 'waiting on the Lord' hoping one day to enjoy life, only to find that the whole time, the Lord is waiting on them! In *Don't Blink* John Merritt uses entertaining stories and biblical insights that give us permission to enjoy life in Christ now—and to dream of a more fulfilling future."

—**Scott Ridout**, President of Converge Worldwide.

"Spending time with John always surpasses my expectations, and as you read *Don't Blink* your expectations will be surpassed as well. What is revealed inside is what a life fully committed to God looks like and, believe it or not, having fun living that life. It's a must read."

—**William Sands**, DDS, Vice Chairperson at UOP Arthur A. Dugoni School of Dentistry.

"I'll never forget the first time I read John Merritt's whale story. It's unforgettable, but then so is John. He lives an adventurous life, but he has doable adventures. You just have to decide to pull out of your safe harbor and get that hook ready for something really big. Why not let *Don't Blink* be your guide to a freshly alive unforgettable life? Don't let this be the one that got away!"

—**Susy Flory**, New York Times Best Selling Author.

"I've known John Merritt as a spiritual leader, teacher, mentor and confidant. John is a person who is able to translate a visionary future into digestible steps so that we're able to be on the journey with him. He will forever be an advisor and leader in my world."

—**Erna Grasz**, CEO of Asante Africa Foundation.

"John Merritt has been with me on hikes through the rainforest, snorkeling adventures in choppy waters, and morning prayers in Jerusalem. The character trait that shines through it all is John's deep and abiding faith. *Don't Blink* shares how this faith informs and guides his passion for life. We can all learn from his insights."
—**Roy Goble**, President & Co-Founder
of PathLight International.

"Grounded but not tethered describes my friend John Merritt. Some pastors ask, 'Are you saved?' John asks that and more. His life asks, 'Are you alive?'
—**James Schaude**, National Accounts Manager, Anixter.

"First my pastor and then good friend, John Merritt's Sunday messages took me from an intimidating relationship with God to a joyful one, while proving how such an ancient book as the Bible can help us lead our best lives. I'm certain you'll discover within these pages that John is 'one of us', easy to relate to and has a sense of humor you'll appreciate.
—**Shelley Rittenbach**, Owner/Partner, Allied Construction
Services.

"John Merritt is a follower of Christ who has impacted thousands of lives as the founding pastor of the resource and refuge known as CrossWinds Church in the San Francisco East Bay. John's leadership has not only been in the context of a pastor but as a creation of God, and he seeks to help all of us take full advantage of the life created for our enjoyment."
—**Robert Sakogawa**, Risk Management Professional.

"John Merritt's zest for living life is what opened the door for me to become all that God had in mind. As a participant with John on several adventures, I've seen how he tackles them head on. Life is meant to be lived fully and John is the embodiment of that reality."

—**Carole Taylor**, Community Life Pastor, CrossWinds Church.

"John Merritt explains how Jesus came to give us abundant life but how often we have reduced the Christian life to a list of 'do's and don'ts.' John has done his research, not in a library, but in the doing of life and he invites us into that adventure. Being his friend for 25 years, I can attest to John's passion for squeezing every ounce out of the wonderful world God has made for us to enjoy."

—**Emily Nelson**, Author and Speaker.

"Whether in a rubber raft in the Icy Straight in Alaska or in a duck blind in the marshlands of the Sacramento Delta, one always feels God's presence and true joy when on an adventure with John Merritt. It has been my pleasure to enjoy a lifetime of adventurous pursuits with my pastor and true friend John."

—**Chris Gullick**, DDS and Co-Founder of CAD3D Academy.

"When a man profoundly changes another man's life for the better, wisdom is always involved. When the same man changes a vast number of lives, the hand of God is involved. John Merritt is such a man."

—**Steve Iversen**, Owner of CU HomeLand Corporation.

"There are many ways to worship God. One of the most satisfying to God must be to enjoy the gift of life and his amazing creation to the fullest extent possible. This being the case, following John's approach to life must really be pleasing to God!"

—**Robert Petersen**, Retired Rocket Scientist.

"Whether we're running ridges, diving for abalone, hunting or floating down the Grand Canyon, John and I experienced many great adventures together. I've looked forward to the release of *Don't Blink* and the encouragement to 'go big' before you 'go home'.

—**Scott Jerlow**, Dive Master and Elk Hunting Guide.

"Most people are content to live their lives in the happy middle. But a few break from the masses and seek the outer edges of adventure and extreme. All my brushes with death have come from following my older brother, John—but so have my brushes with pure exhilaration and glory. I was fortunate to be able to tag along with one of the most uninhibited, adventurous and genuinely free spirits I have ever known. John showed me a better and bolder way to attack life and I will forever love him for that.

—**Bob Merritt**, Senior Pastor of
Eagle Brook Church and Author of Get Wise.

don't blink

The Life You Won't Want To Miss

john merritt

New York

don't blink

The Life You Won't Want To Miss

Published in New York, New York, by Morgan James Publishing. Morgan James and The Entrepreneurial Publisher are trademarks of Morgan James, LLC.
www.MorganJamesPublishing.com

The Morgan James Speakers Group can bring authors to your live event. For more information or to book an event visit The Morgan James Speakers Group at www.TheMorganJamesSpeakersGroup.com.

Scripture quotations marked (NIV®) are taken from the HOLY BIBLE, NEW INTERNATIONAL VERSION ®. NIV®. Copyright © 1973, 1978, 1984, 2011 by Biblica, Inc.®. Used by permission. All rights reserved worldwide.

A **free** eBook edition is available with the purchase of this print book.

CLEARLY PRINT YOUR NAME ABOVE IN UPPER CASE

Instructions to claim your free eBook edition:
1. Download the BitLit app for Android or iOS
2. Write your name in **UPPER CASE** on the line
3. Use the BitLit app to submit a photo
4. Download your eBook to any device

ISBN 978-1-63047-561-1 paperback
ISBN 978-1-63047-562-8 eBook
Library of Congress Control Number:
2015901751

Cover Design by:
Rachel Lopez
www.r2cdesign.com

Interior Design by:
Bonnie Bushman
bonnie@caboodlegraphics.com

In an effort to support local communities and raise awareness and funds, Morgan James Publishing donates a percentage of all book sales for the life of each book to Habitat for Humanity Peninsula and Greater Williamsburg.

Get involved today, visit
www.MorganJamesBuilds.com

Habitat
for Humanity®
Peninsula and
Greater Williamsburg
Building Partner

dedication

To my devoted wife Debbie, to our esteemed children Aaron (and wife Gretchen), Nathan (and wife Jenn), and Julia; to our cherished grandchildren Abigail, Brady, Callie, Logan, Reese (and those yet to come); to my fearless father Cal, and to my loving mother Barb…Also to good friends who share my spirit of adventure—many of whom were either willing or naïve enough to accompany me into the great unknown.

table of contents

foreword

For years I've taken it on the chin as a pastor for using 1 Timothy 6:17b to justify my love for Cuban cigars and fine wine, especially the part that says God ". . . richly provides us with everything for our enjoyment." Sure, I know that the Great Apostle Paul most likely did not have a vintage Cabernet or Cohiba in mind when he wrote those words, but in my estimation they fill the theological bill.

Our God is not only gracious but good, and his children feel His pleasure when they seriously *enjoy* his goodness in their lives. That's the fundamental principle so skillfully, humorously, biblically, profoundly, and practically laid out in this wonderful book by my dear friend John Merritt.

Don't Blink: The Life You Won't Want to Miss is a desperately needed corrective to the false notion inflicted upon generations of believers that following Christ is, by definition, a grim and somber affair bereft of pleasure but obese with duty. Do Christian disciples have duties to fulfill? Sure! But we should always fulfill our duties with the hilariously reassuring perspective that no one is more delighted by joyfully fulfilled lives than our Heavenly Father.

Jesus did say, after all, that He came that we might live *more abundant* lives! The beautiful thing about this book is that it shows John Merritt not only believes Jesus' promise, but has *experienced* it. The 23 personal, true-life stories that he recounts prove it, and will make you want to believe Jesus' promise and prove it too!

I know this because John, as my fellow pastor and friend and sporadic golfing buddy (because he lives in California and I live in Texas) has been having that effect on my life for almost two decades now. I don't know anyone who laughs more, loves more, lives more, enjoys more, serves more, or gives more than my friend. And all that not in spite of being a follower of Christ, but because of it!

You are in for a treat by reading this book because in each chapter John not only rolls out the biblical elements of a fulfilled, joyful, happy life, but also shows how this plays out in the real world. He is transparent about his faults (which makes you love him), authentic about his failures (which makes you believe him), and exuberant about his joy (which makes you follow him). A great example to which I can give personal confirmation is John's "Clint Eastwood" story in Chapter 11 where he writes:

"Slow down, man," my friend said. "Look at the gait of the guy on the left. Doesn't he look familiar?" I took a closer look at the slender guy with the grayish hair strolling along, and then it hit me. "No! Can't be! Is it really?" "Sure is. We just hit all four of our golf balls over Clint Eastwood's head!" my buddy said.

True confession time: it is my dubious honor to be John's "friend" in this story (sorry Mr. Eastwood, but it really was John's fault this ever happened!). So when John talks about "grabbing hold of grace", I can attest that he *actually* does. You can also take it to the bank when John talks about *"only one life"* and *"there's nothing like love"* and *"no reason to fear"* and *"always a reason to hope"*. This is joy in real time, experience not theory, truth not fiction, gift not burden.

One last thing. When John writes that *"there is no someday"* please understand that he is giving us the rationale for righteously grabbing all the gusto out of life today. Having just survived a gnarly bout with stage four colon cancer, I can bear witness to the wisdom of that perspective. We do only have this one life, and God calls us to live it to the full. Time's a wasting! So I'm excited that you're reading this book. *Don't Blink* will definitely help you live the life you don't want to miss!

—**Dr. Andy McQuitty**, Senior Pastor of Irving Bible Church, and author of *Notes from the Valley: A Spiritual Cancer Travelogue.*

acknowledgments

I wish to thank the CrossWinds Church Family who gave me the freedom to pursue the adventures that energize my life, and for allowing me to break just about every stereotype of who people think a pastor should be.

Thanks to all my friends and family who encouraged me to write, including my siblings Kathy, Bob, Debbie and Jan.

A special thanks to my agents Alice Crider (now with Cook Publishing) and Greg Johnson with WordServe Literary, who share my passion for life and chose to promote my work due to their strong belief in the message of this book.

To Susy Flory, best-selling author and friend who encouraged me to hang in there when the going was tough—thank you.

To Karen O'Connor, who served as my first editor, and who I didn't like for a while because she was so ruthless—thank you for making me a better writer.

Also to the fine people at Morgan James Publishing—to Terry Whalin for picking up my book, to company founder David Hancock for championing the relevance of my words, to Tiffany Gibson for her professional navigation through all the editing details, and to Nickcole Watkins for her expertise in marketing.

Finally, I am extremely grateful for so many friends who have enriched my life through the years—some named in this book but many more unnamed. I am forever thankful for the joy, the laughter and the shared experiences that have made my life complete.

introduction

"At judgment day every man will have to give an account for every good thing which he might have enjoyed, and did not."

(Rabbinic saying)

For the record, there is no eleventh commandment that says: "Thou shalt not enjoy life." Nor does God ever say, "My plan for you is to be miserable on earth until you arrive in heaven." What the Bible does say is that God *"…richly provides us with everything for our enjoyment."* (I Timothy 6:17b) In other words, God has given us an amazing world to enjoy—so what's holding us back from living a life that's deeply satisfying?

You are invited to join me on a pilgrimage of adventure that will address some common obstacles to living an exhilarating life. When Jesus said, *"I have come that they may have life and have it to the full,"* (John 10:10b) he wasn't talking about waiting until we get to heaven. Jesus was pointing to a God-oriented life where we are thriving as fully alive human beings. The earth reflects a joyful Creator who gives us his creation for our pleasure. Heaven and earth are converging in stunning fashion all around us, and we have the opportunity to seize the day in all of its infinite possibilities. I hope there is not one piece of that life you want to miss out on.

There are several misconceptions about the Christian life I will address in this book. One false impression is that when you become a Christian, you are required to give up much of what you find satisfying and your fun is over. Truth is, God maximizes our ability to enjoy life and gives us unlimited freedom to live the most fulfilling lives possible. If there is any sin in this, it is in our reluctance to consider how God can raise the quality of our lives to new levels of fulfillment and joy.

Another misconception is that if you are enjoying life you had better feel guilty about it. I understand where this notion comes from. We see others who are less fortunate in terms of material wealth and we wonder if it is right for us to have nice things and do what gives us pleasure. This is a healthy tension and the matter of stewardship must be considered. But instead of feeling guilty, the appropriate response to all God provides is one of gratitude. Life is a gift given to us each day to be opened and enjoyed with grateful hearts. And when this causes us to smile, we can be sure God is smiling too.

The chapters that follow contain twenty-one true-life stories that will take you to places as diverse as Alaska, Argentina and the Amazon in situations ranging from dangerous to humorous. Many of the narratives describe life-threatening situations due to inherent degrees of risk and uncertain outcomes. But this really describes what life is like when God is leading the charge—audacious, extraordinary, unconventional, and hardly a dull moment. As we become courageous enough to follow, our intimacy with God deepens. Life is never the same, never boring, and always awaiting the next great adventure.

I don't think any of us want to look back on our lives with regret about what might have been. My hope is that God would become your life-elevating force, refusing to settle for anything less than the quest God has for you. Each chapter ends with several questions for reflection and discussion. The questions will help you think about times when you may have settled for a smaller version of life, an easier path, or a safer route that has left you less than satisfied. The questions will also help you think about what life might look like and where it might take you if God was more of an intimate partner in your voyage.

So let the journey begin! May these pages be like an ocean breeze that clears the fog, providing a splash of courage to your spirit, and injecting some vigor into your veins. If you feel like you are stuck on a reef and not sure how to get off, I trust that the following chapters will help you start sailing again. And if you are used to catching guppies instead of whales, that is about to change!

Toward the noble quest of boldly pursuing all that life has to offer, *let's get on with it!*

"Receive every day as a resurrection from death, as a new enjoyment of life; meet every rising sun with such sentiments of God's goodness, as if you had seen it, and all things, new-created upon your account: and under the sense of so great a blessing, let your joyful heart praise and magnify so good and glorious a Creator."

—William Law

humpbacks

It's Good to Be Alive

have you ever smelled whale breath? I have and it's the nastiest stench ever! A forty-ton monster snuck up on me and my buddy while fishing, surfacing a mere thirty feet from our boat. Sounding like an explosion, the misty air came blasting out of his blow hole. Being downwind, we were treated to the putrid smell of rotted fish. Worst case of halitosis ever!

Though I have been on hundreds of fishing trips, I've never left the dock thinking I'd be close enough to a whale to smell his breath. And never have I entertained the ridiculous notion of hooking a whale. But I've learned that once you venture out to sea and put your line in the water, unexpected events can and do occur—events that are not possible when at home sitting on a couch.

On one particular voyage, we found the ocean so calm and flat you could have water skied the twenty-five miles from the Golden Gate Bridge to the Farallon Islands. Once we throttled down over our favorite fishing spot, there was an eerie sort of quiet that felt quite strange, even spooky for a wild and unpredictable ocean. Of course, it's always a bit unnerving when you're so far off shore you can no longer see land.

That day the waters around the Farallons were bursting with a spectacular array of life. Diving sea birds and leaping porpoises chased huge schools of bait fish. Best of all, countless whales joined in on the ocean buffet, dining on massive bands of shrimp-like crustaceans called "krill."

Seeing Gray Whales off the California coast is a fairly common occurrence as they migrate between Alaskan and Mexican waters. But today we were surrounded by Humpbacks! As the day rolled on, we realized not a minute went by without seeing or hearing a whale blowing, breaching, spy-hopping, or slapping their flukes.

Toward the end of the day I was trying to catch one more ling cod. While bouncing my jig in ninety feet of water, I looked up and saw two whales surface less than 100 yards away. They blew several times as they swam directly toward the boat. At less than fifty yards away I announced to my friend, "Hey man, we've got a couple of whales coming right at us."

I set my fishing pole down against the side rail and reached for my camera. But before I could snap a photo, the whales flipped their tails and took a dive directly under the boat.

When I picked up my pole, there was something heavy tugging on my line. I pulled back, setting the hook, and my pole doubled over. I thought for a moment I was snagged on the bottom because the pull was so strong. But no! Line began racing out of the reel, and there was no stopping it.

Then, instead of being pulled in a downward direction, the line started moving horizontally. No question about it, whatever I had on the end of the line was coming up.

I looked to the other side where my line was stretched out, as the whale surfaced, blew, and continued to swim away from me, *taking my line with it!* With the sixty-pound test fishing line screaming off my reel, I yelled, "Hey Steve, look! I caught a whale! Can you believe this?"

I let this massive creature pull out a few more yards of line, and then decided that I would be a good sportsman and practice "catch and release." I tightened the drag, the line broke, and the behemoth was gone. In a dazed state of mind, I collapsed on the deck, trying to verify that I wasn't hallucinating.

As I watched those two humpbacks blasting air and swimming off toward Maui, one with my hook in his mouth, I laughed out loud. While gazing at the western horizon I thought to myself, *Nothing can top this! Not a shark, not a tuna, not a marlin—nothing!*

It suddenly occurred to me that I had just reached the apex of my fishing career. And now, any time I hear someone bragging about the fish he caught, I have the perfect line: "Ever caught a whale?"

• • • • •

I've replayed this rare moment at sea countless times. I don't know what you call a miracle, but how does a 165-pound man on one end of a thin line become attached to an 80,000 pound animal on the other end of that line by way of dangling a small hook in an infinite abyss? Whether you see that as a miracle, or just a one in a trillion chance and I got lucky, the fact that it happened has caused me to use one particular word a lot less often. That word is "impossible."

People often stop pursuing their dreams when too much weight is given to pragmatism. Maybe you have heard someone in your life use the word "impossible" so often that it's caused you to stop dreaming. Granted, I did not go out fishing that day in late November thinking I was going to hook a whale. But I also know this about fishing—if your boat stays in the harbor, and you never wet your line, you aren't going to catch anything. On the other hand, if you push off from the docks, get out to where the fish are and make a cast, all kinds of new possibilities come up.

I am still shocked that a whale swam into my dangling hook. But that experience, among many others, causes me to ask you a question you may have never considered before—why settle for a fish when you can hook a whale? Settling for fish is no longer of interest once you realize hooking a whale is possible and you discover how *alive* it makes you feel.

Certainly there are those days when you venture out with the highest hopes of filling your coolers full of wild krill-fed salmon, and you can already taste the fresh filet grilling on your barbecue. But that day everything that can go wrong does go wrong, like it has on any number of our days at sea. We've had our expensive marine navigation equipment stop working with no land in sight. Boat engines have overheated, run poorly, and stopped suddenly, leaving us dead in the water. Some days we've limped into the harbor completely discouraged and wondering why we do this. Why do we? Because there will be another day—a day when magic can happen.

Too many of us seem to resemble the vast majority of boats that remain shackled to the docks in the safety of the harbor, growing barnacles on the bottom side and moss on the topside. But what a thing of beauty when the engines are humming or the sail is unfurled and the hull graces the water like a dancer waltzing across the floor. As you read, I hope you will hear the beckoning call to cast off your restraints, glide out of the harbor and discover all the open sea called *life* has to give you. We were created with the God-given freedom to explore, take risks, live life to the full, and chase our dreams with passion. Along the way, I pray that you will discover the greatest adventure of all—God's life becoming more of your life.

• • • • •

Sometimes we drop crab pots in the water on our way out to the fishing grounds, let them soak for several hours, and pull the pots up on our way back to the dock. In my estimation, there is nothing better in all the world than steamed Dungeness Crab dipped in melted butter and garlic, along with fresh sourdough bread, Caesar salad on the side, all washed down with a crisp sauvignon blanc. I remember saying to my wife as I was stuffing another pile of crab leg sweetness into my mouth, "It doesn't get any better than this."

And then as I sat there feasting and reflecting on an invigorating day at sea, I looked across the table at Debbie and said, "You know honey, it's good to be alive!" And she nodded in agreement and said, "Yes, it certainly is!"

Can you remember the last time you said that? When was the last time you either said out loud, or at least thought to yourself, *It's good to be alive?* What were you doing? What was it about the moment or the experience that lead you to say or think that? I would ask that you to lift you head up from the words on this page right now, and try to identify a specific time that caused you to exclaim, *It's good to be alive!*

Ponder this: Do you think God is worried? Despairing? Frowning? Full of angst and dread? Of course not! Don't you think God enjoys all of creation every single moment in ways that we cannot even begin to comprehend? Imagine how much pleasure God finds in the beauty and complexity of the universe that continually dances before him. I wonder if we have lost sight of this aspect of who God is, what God enjoys, and how we were made to enjoy what he does. I believe God delights with us when we are pulling up crab pots, or doing whatever it is that causes us to say, *It's good to be alive!* As David declares in poetic fashion: *"You make known to me the path of life, you will fill me with joy in your presence, with eternal pleasures at your right hand."* (Psalm 16:11)

You may not be the adventurous type and are disinterested in a full-fledged venture at sea. May I encourage you to begin by untying your boat from the dock for a gentle cruise around the harbor? If you are going through a difficult season of life, and living life to the full seems too much for you, I propose that you can live a larger life one day at a time. Even if you never plan to ride a motorcycle, strap on diving gear or ski down a mountainside, I hope you will discover what will assist you in making the most of your everyday life. I believe everyone can find a passion that fits who they are, whether paddling through whitewater or enjoying a back yard barbecue with good friends.

That said, when you find yourself laying face-down on the pavement like I have, surviving life takes precedence over enjoying life. But these are times when God can get an urgent message through that needs to reach our ears—maybe a message that says there is no someday, only *this* day. More about that in the next chapter...

It's Good to Be Alive...

- Would you describe your life more as a boat at rest in the harbor or as a ship under sail in the open sea?

- What dreams or goals have you been putting off because you think they are unrealistic or because someone has told you they are impossible to achieve?
- Do your dreams align with your passions? To determine this, ask yourself what activity, hobby, job or pursuit makes you feel most fully alive.
- What "whale-sized" challenge in your life will require some courage in order for you to move forward? Consider taking a moment right now to ask God for help in navigating a course through what may be uncharted waters.

2 crash landing
Only One Life

t he minute hand on the soot-covered clock inside the Western Pennsylvania steel mill moved slowly. The July humidity combined with the heat of the mammoth furnaces used to shape and roll steel created sweltering working conditions. But the job would help pay for my college tuition, and provided an unexpected incentive to complete my education.

Finally the three o'clock siren blew and I was out of there. I hopped on my motorcycle, sped home for a quick shower, strapped a duffle bag to the back of my bike and roared down the road with a whoop and a shout! From the dungeon of the mill to the freedom of the open road! My spirit soared.

The destination was paradise. My parents were vacationing on Hilton Head Island, South Carolina in a luxurious beach home. I couldn't wait to get down there to join them. But I had 950 miles to cover before I would feel the sand between my toes and the surf around my ankles. It was time to make tracks.

Things were going well as I crossed the Pennsylvania border into Maryland. The scene in my rearview mirror was as pretty as a postcard with the sun creating an orange glow on the horizon. Life was good. I was all smiles—there were bugs in my teeth! Everything was going as planned, except for a minor irritant that was causing a bit of concern as I put mile after mile behind me.

Two of the little bolts that attached the fender to the front fork were loose and were causing my front fender to vibrate. My haste to keep moving overcame common sense. Instead of stopping, I elected to lean forward with my chest resting on my gas tank. With one hand on the throttle I reached down with my other hand in an attempt to tighten the bolt—while going 70 miles per hour down a four-lane freeway.

Quicker than my eye could see, the bottom edge of my fender caught the rotating front tire of my motorcycle and instantly locked up the front wheel. With the front tire no longer rotating, the motorcycle lost stability and flipped on its side. I was slammed to the pavement so hard and so fast that I didn't even feel the initial impact.

As I flipped onto the asphalt, a vague awareness came over me. I had just wiped out and was lying on a freeway somewhere in Maryland.

Dazed and confused, I stumbled off the right lane of the freeway and staggered onto the shoulder. Somehow I was able to gather my wits enough to walk up to where my beloved *Honda 350* lay wrapped around the guardrail.

A car had pulled up behind me. A woman got out shouting. She had been right behind my motorcycle and saw me wipe out. "Are you all right? Do you need help? I can't believe you survived!"

"Yeah, I think I'm ok," I mumbled. That was the last I remember of her.

By now I was feeling the bruises starting to throb but not enough to stop me from getting my hands underneath the bike and setting it upright. A superficial assessment revealed a number of minor damages, but most critical was the crumpled front fender wedged between the front forks and the tire.

Only after looking my bike over did I look at myself. As far as I could tell there were no broken bones, no bleeding, no paralysis, and most miraculous of all, not a scratch on my helmet. There were several raw and inflamed wounds on my left side where initial contact with the pavement peeled away at least one layer of skin.

As daylight faded, I got out my small tool kit and struggled to work the fender free from between the front forks. Within a few minutes I accomplished that task. I then straddled what was left of my motorcycle, put my foot on the kick-start, and it started up on the first try. I was headed back down the road. I thought about looking for a hospital, but found a campground with a hot shower instead. I was still shaking from the shock as I cleansed my tender wounds.

I didn't sleep very well that night, but that didn't matter. I remember lying in my sleeping bag and looking up into a black sky flooded with stars. Never before had the night sky seemed so stunning. My mind was a jumble of thoughts as I reflected on the events of the day. *How close was that car behind me as I flip-flopped on the pavement? Why wasn't I run over? How could I get up and walk away? Why was there no evidence of my helmet hitting the pavement? Was there a guardian angel looking out for me?* The answers remain a mystery, although I am inclined to believe the answer to the last question is *yes*.

• • • • •

This turned out to be a major life-shaping event that, first of all, filled me with a sense of gratitude. I gazed at the stars and thanked God to be alive. He could have taken me that day, but he didn't. For whatever reason, he allowed my life to continue. I could only conclude that God had a greater purpose for my life—something more than riding motorcycles, making money and chasing girls.

Perhaps you've found yourself gazing into the vast night sky and sensed there is a greater, undiscovered purpose for your life. Maybe you have emerged from a life-threatening experience with a strong belief in something larger, something more significant that God wants to show you. He reminds us that there are no guarantees about how long or how healthy or how complete our lives will be. We are wise to make the most of each day on earth while we can because *today* is all we have—there really is no *someday*. Yesterday is gone and tomorrow may never come—now is the time to seek out the life God has planned for us.

But first, there is something God wants us to know when a smooth ride turns into a crash landing. After flipping my motorcycle, I knew God was there, picking me up off the pavement. Along with the certainty of God's presence was the conviction that my life mattered to him. I felt his warm embrace as I gazed into the heavens that sleepless night. Even in my pain, I felt God's compassion.

I'm wondering if you know this about God—that your life matters to him too. There may be reasons why you might think you don't matter much to God. Perhaps you're facing a serious situation and you wonder if God cares because he is not responding to your cries for help. When you find yourself face down on the highway of life, you may conclude that God is either apathetic about your existence or that he is really ticked off. Please know that nothing could be further from the truth. God does not delight in tragedy, nor does he seek to smack us into submission when we're not paying attention. That is not the way God operates.

God draws near to us during times when we may be most receptive to making a human-divine connection. You may have never wiped out on a motorcycle, but perhaps you've survived a car crash that could've taken your life. You may have beaten the odds in a bout with cancer, or recovered from a serious heart attack. Maybe you've served in the military and escaped with your life but not without battle wounds. Most of us can think of incidents in our growing up years where we could have died or have been maimed for life. But we've lived to tell about it.

God doesn't send catastrophe to let us know who's in charge. Sometimes things happen to challenge the presumption that we will be just fine on our own—that God is needed only in case of emergency. When life slams us on the pavement, God makes his presence known by coming alongside to get us back on our feet. As we allow him to assist us in putting the pieces back together, he also has a way of opening our eyes to his greater purpose for our existence.

• • • • •

In the Gospels, we find the story of a man named Matthew who found himself stunned by the fact that Jesus would show any interest in him. One day as Matthew was at work at his lucrative job of collecting taxes, Jesus came up to him and simply said, "Follow me." There was something about Jesus that compelled Matthew to drop everything he was doing that moment and follow Jesus. Later we find Jesus having dinner at Matthew's house in the company of Matthew's friends who had reputations that were less than admirable. When Jesus was criticized by the religious types for hanging out with "sinners" the likes of Matthew and his buddies, Jesus told his critics that the mission of his life was to seek out those who needed God the most, not those who needed God the least. (Matthew 9:9-13)

The truth is that long before we ever decided to go on a search for God, God was on a search for us. What interests God more than anything else is to connect or reconnect with men and women who have become skilled at excluding him from their lives. Jesus yearns to meet those wanting a more vital connection with God but who might be confused about how that can happen. Jesus' mission was to show us that living a God-directed life leads to better outcomes than living life on our own.

Even now you may be hearing Jesus saying, *Come, follow me.* I hope you will take that risky step and allow Jesus to show you what living God's adventure means for you. Don't hesitate. There is nothing to fear. Jesus has nothing but good in mind for your life. Take him up on his invitation and he will begin to unveil a plan for your life that goes far beyond anything you could have imagined. I urge you not to resist God's initiatives but to welcome and embrace them.

As I lay there in that campground, looking up at the stars, I did something that I don't often do. I cried. I cried because I was trembling, because I was in pain, because I was alone, because I was scared, and ironically, because I knew God was there. It was both a comforting and a frightening experience. That is usually the way it is when God draws near. But I knew beyond all doubt that I was hearing him say, *Follow me.* I was not just saying *ok* to that appeal, I was running into his arms.

Jesus always meets you where you are, on your own turf, in your own life situation, and lets you know that you matter very much to him. He comes with open arms for all who need his strong embrace. And if you are ready to follow him, you are in for the greatest adventure of your lives.

Only One Life...

- Identify a serious crisis or a near death experience that you may have been through. What purpose, if any, have you been able to discern from that experience?

- Do you feel that life has "slammed you to the pavement" in some way? Have you had difficulty recovering from this experience, or has this served to "get you down the road" toward a new direction for your life?

- In what ways, if any, do you think that your past experiences are holding you back from moving forward with God's greater plans for your life?

- What is it that you often use the word "someday" to describe something that you intend to do or accomplish? What is it that you need to go after or get started *today*?

- If you can, name a time when you felt God's embrace—a time when you knew you deeply mattered to him.

3

spread eagle
There Is No Someday

W atching our worship pastor suspended over the water like a hovering crow worried me. I had no intention of hurting him. But when a harmonic convergence of water came together and launched him, I saw a catastrophe in the making.

Ten of us boat drivers provide tube and wakeboard rides for 200 students every year at our week-long High School Houseboat Trip. Safety is a priority but mishaps are inevitable. Like the kid with braces who was bouncing around while seated on a banana tube and sank his teeth into the back of the head of the kid in front of him. Ouch! A trip to the hospital and several stitches later and he was fine.

But that was nothing compared to what happened to Pastor Josh. He held on valiantly while the boat whipped him around in a circle. A second circle created a vortex of waves heaping up like a churning caldron. I then did a quick figure eight, hurling Josh across the mound of water. He hit the liquid launching pad perfectly, rocketing all 230 pounds of his body into space.

Josh let go of the tube at the apex of his ascent, and in a full spread eagle, began his descent from a height well above the wake board tower. He hit the water with a resounding belly-flop and lay there like a dead seal.

For a few moments he did not lift his head. *Oh no! I just killed our Worship Pastor!*

I raced the boat over to where he was floating. "Are you all right?" I yelled. He moaned as two guys jumped in and dragged him to the swim step. That is when Josh noticed his shorts were split open from front to back leaving him completely exposed. When he saw this he chuckled, but a jolt of pain turned the chuckle into a groan.

He cried out in agony as we helped him into the boat. Even a gentle push or pull caused him to grimace. I feared something was seriously wrong. We held up a towel so the girls wouldn't witness what we were witnessing—more of Josh than we cared to see! We tried to be empathetic but part of this scene was very funny.

Once seated in the boat we did our best to make him comfortable. After catching his breath, Josh spoke his first words. "That was so worth it! That was one of the coolest things I've ever done in my entire life."

I smiled to myself. *Josh, you need to get out more.*

His pain increased that day so he was taken by boat to the hospital. The doctors determined the cartilage holding his ribs in place had been torn, separating his rib cage from his sternum. He would live with pain for several more weeks, but eventually his ribs would reattach themselves and he would be fine.

• • • • •

Wouldn't you agree that life is a mixture of joy and pain, laughter and agony? One moment we're flying high and on top of the world. The next moment we're crashing hard, not sure if we'll sink or swim.

Every year we see this in the lives of the students who come to Lake Shasta eager to have a good time. They arrive ready for fun but they also bring their brokenness with them. Smiling and confident on the outside, they carry wounds on the inside. Sometimes it's the bad choices they've made that haunt them. Others are hurting due to the separation of their parents. Many are lonely and have feelings of rejection. These young people often shed tears as they open up and talk about their lives.

Watching frowns turn to smiles inspires the adults as students discover new ways to live life. Many learn for the first time what a personal relationship with Jesus looks like. Every year dozens of kids invite Christ into their lives to be their Savior, God, and Friend. Those who are doing drugs or having sex often find a better way of living with God as their guiding light.

Never in our nineteen years of taking students to the lake had we been struck by a real tragedy except for year sixteen. Jeremiah was a twenty-year-old son of an adoptive father. He had participated in Houseboats on Lake Shasta during his high school years, and became a committed Christian. He now was serving as one of the adult co-leaders.

Jeremiah's zeal for life matched his passion for God, expressed by a faith best described as bold, expressive and authentic. His life was a great example of what *seize the day* meant. But his youthful sense of invincibility sometimes propelled him to take unwise risks.

Hardly anyone knew Jeremiah was climbing into a dry suit at about ten o'clock the first morning of Houseboats 2009. This was designated quiet time when the students were scattered about in solitude. Meanwhile, our young leader was entering the water.

A certified scuba diver always probes the water directly behind the rafted-up houseboats to make sure it's clear of underwater hazards. No more scuba diving is permitted once that task is completed. A rumor began floating around that Jeremiah was missing, and that someone last saw him in the water with scuba gear forty-five minutes earlier. Our leaders immediately verified this disturbing report was true. A few students on shore had been watching the bubbles on the surface from Jeremiah's air tank.

Within minutes, over 200 sets of eyes scanned the water where Jeremiah was last seen. By controlled breathing a skilled diver can swim for up to an hour on one tank of air. Time was running out. Without any further hesitation, we dialed 911 and requested urgent assistance in finding a lost diver.

Within minutes a sheriff's patrol boat arrived, joined by three search and rescue boats equipped with sophisticated sonar and a team of professional divers. We couldn't believe our eyes. Was this really happening? Watching a search and rescue operation for one of our friends was unbearable for many of the students. Tears flowed and prayers were sent heavenward.

Hour after hour dragged on while leaders did their best to provide support for the students. Some of the teens were quiet and reflective. Others poured out their grief. Conversations about life and about God took on greater relevance and deeper meaning.

Houseboats 2009 would come to a premature close the following morning. Our final worship service that evening took on a serious tone. An aura of authenticity was evident in our worship, our words and our prayers. Jeremiah's father (serving as an adult leader) spoke courageously to the students. "Remember the faith and confidence Jeremiah had in his Lord and Savior, Jesus Christ. If he were here, you know that he would want you to declare Jesus as your Savior too," he said. God's Spirit seemed to be hovering over these precious students. Many made life-shaping decisions that night.

Mercifully, the divers pulled Jeremiah's lifeless body out of the water about 100 yards down the shore as darkness descended, just after worship had ended. No one will ever know for sure what happened below the surface, but that spot in Little Backbone Bay became a sacred place. The students built an alter of stones and left it behind, along with their good-byes.

The memorial service for Jeremiah filled our 1000-seat church auditorium with adults and students from area high schools. In my message, I referenced the many *why* questions which were difficult or impossible to answer. Why things happen involves a mysterious intersection of God's sovereignty with human choice, coming together in ways often beautiful and tragic at the same time. The writer of Ecclesiastes reminds us: *"There is a time for everything, and a season for every activity under the heavens: a time to be born and a time to die...a time to weep and a time to laugh, a time to mourn and a time to dance* " (Ecclesiastes 3:1, 2, 4)

This is the nature of life—a mixture of joy and pain, laughter and sadness, life and death. One moment we are doing spread eagles behind a boat. The next moment we are mourning over a great loss. In those times, we may wonder if we will ever laugh again. But laughter, even if through tears, will help restore our lives. In the meantime, God waits for us, God weeps with us, and God washes his mercy over us. God understands even when we think he doesn't.

There were many life lessons learned on the lake that summer. We were struck by how vulnerable life is, how it could be over in an instant, and that each day is a gift to be opened and enjoyed. We were glad for the reality of a heaven awaiting those of us who had faith in Jesus like Jeremiah did. But many of us also came away from the lake with a greater intentionality to squeeze every drop out of every day of life God gives us. I hope this will become your resolve as well.

There Is No Someday...

- The Bible says there is a time to laugh and a time to mourn. Describe the last time you did both.
- What question about life or death have you found to be most unanswerable?
- What single event or series of events changed you as a person more than any other?
- What has God revealed to you, if anything, through personal loss?
- Do you find yourself more focused on heaven than what God has for you here and now? What would help you see each day as a gift to be opened and enjoyed?

marijuana smoke
The Search for Meaning

he marijuana smoke hung like a thick ground fog over the wooded lawns of Vandal Park. So many people were smoking pot there was no need to light up. With great intrigue my traveling partner and I inhaled the sweet-smelling air as it drifted through our nostrils on this intoxicating summer evening.

Seven thousand hippies from all over the world were gathered there in Amsterdam. They were a colorful bunch in their tie-dyed shirts, beads, rings, sandals, long hair and a long time between showering. And looking back, we fit in pretty well—the hair, the bib overalls, the back packs, the whole catastrophe.

My college buddy, Dean, and I were hitchhiking our way through England, France, Switzerland, Germany, the Netherlands and Belgium. We got our free ticket to Europe by joining our college male choir that had a European singing tour on the summer schedule. Once the concerts were over, the two of us said good-bye to our fellow choir members in London and pointed our thumbs in the direction of the English Channel.

We found most Europeans to be cordial—like the German guy who gave us a lift on his way home from the Spanish Riviera. Instead of dropping us off alongside the road, he invited us to spend the night in his Dusseldorf apartment. When he opened his trunk, he showed us his inventory of liquor he'd purchased while on vacation. Once settled into his apartment, he offered us shots of whiskey, and then took us around town to what seemed like every bar in Dusseldorf. The words *"Nein danke"* did not seem to exist in his vocabulary, and we were relieved that he was able to drive back to his apartment without incident.

Nor will we forget the elderly gray-haired woman who pulled over on the freeway entrance ramp just outside Paris where we were thumbing for a ride. Assuming she had stopped to give us a lift, we opened the back door of her immaculate Mercedes, threw our backpacks inside, and hopped in. We were quite surprised that this dignified and sharply dressed French woman would stop for strangers the likes of us.

Turns out she spoke no English, and Dean's French was woefully inadequate. The woman kept pointing to a map, and we thought she was trying to inquire where the two of us were headed. It wasn't until she took an exit at a rest stop about 100 kilometers down the highway that we found out what was really going on.

She found a young man fluent in both French and English who served as our translator. With wild gestures and rapid-fire French, she told him what the situation was. The young man then turned to us and said, "There is a problem."

"What's the problem?" we asked.

"Well, when this woman stopped on the entrance ramp, it wasn't to pick you up. She was asking for directions! When you jumped into her car, she thought you were up to no good, and were taking advantage of an old woman. For the last 100 kilometers, she had nerve-wracking thoughts about what you two Americans were going to do to her."

We felt terrible. "Tell her we are so sorry, and please apologize for our mistake," we said.

She was relieved to hear our apology translated into French. We sheepishly retrieved our backpacks from her car and said our goodbyes. She wasted no time in driving off with a wild story to tell. I was sure she wouldn't be stopping to ask for directions any time soon.

Two weeks later, we found ourselves in the Netherlands among a mass of youthful humanity. All of us were searching— seeking meaning, seeking direction, seeking a vision for a better world—or simply escaping from whatever we felt was restricting our personal freedoms.

Kindling the search was the confusion of the Viet Nam War where members of our generation were shedding blood in a conflict we considered senseless. My draft number was 71, and was it not for a student deferment, I may have been slogging my way through the swamps of Southeast Asia instead of touring the Heineken Brewery.

Unfortunately, our rendezvous in Amsterdam resulted in a deeper sense of confusion. Looting was rampant in the park. People were stealing from one another and the crime rate was high. A pervasive aura of aimlessness and despondency hung over this place as thick as the cloud of marijuana.

What kind of new community is this I wondered? What kind of value system? People were desperate. While rejecting the materialism of our parents' generation we found that the pendulum swinging in a direction that was even more unattractive and troublesome. What bothered me most was our collective hypocrisy. In rebelling against a society full of maddening inconsistencies, we found ourselves caught up in a society worse than the one we had rejected.

And so, we walked away from the smoldering joints, the strumming guitars and the gloomy despair of that place with fewer answers and more questions. We didn't know where the next bend in the road would take us, but there was no way that we were going to settle for what was being offered there.

• • • • •

Have you ever felt like a hitchhiker on a spiritual journey? You want to make progress and you want God's guidance—but you're not sure when your next ride is coming or where it will take you. Maybe your road map is marked up with detours and dead ends. If so, do not despair. You are not alone.

Most all of us have in mind a general road map for our lives that may include education, career, family, and hopefully a measure of satisfaction along the way. What we actually discover is the road from London to Amsterdam is filled with unexpected twists and turns that shape and define our lives. Some seasons of life are like a long smooth ride from Paris to the Riviera. Other seasons feel like you are standing alongside a road with your thumb out while you're stuck eating dust as car after car roars past you as if you don't exist.

I've also found that there are certain constants in life's journey— like that sometimes intangible yet insatiable yearning for something more, something better, something interesting enough to keep us motivated and engaged. Part of what it means to be a fully alive human being is refusing to stagnate in an unsatisfactory mode of existence, but always looking down the road for greater meaning and fulfillment out of the years allotted to us. We know we have just one shot at this, and the last thing we want to do is come to the end of our lives with a lot of disappointment over what might have been.

We can assume this is why Abraham (or Abram) was so responsive when God showed up and gave him these instructions: *"Go from your country, your people and your father's household to the land I will show you."* And how did Abraham respond? *"So Abram went, as the Lord had told him."* (Genesis 12:1, 4a)

This was a big deal. God is directing Abram to uproot his family, depart from his homeland, and leave all that is familiar behind. This was no small endeavor for this man at seventy-five years of age.

Where was this land God was directing him to find? In hindsight we know that he was being sent to the beautiful land of Canaan. But the reality of his situation is revealed toward the end of the Bible where Abraham is recognized for his faith. *"By faith Abraham, when called to go to a place he would later receive as his inheritance, obeyed and went, even though he did not know where he was going."* (Hebrews 11:8)

That took some courage and trust. Imagine Abraham's friends asking, "So Abe, where you headed?"

"Not sure."

"But you must have a destination in mind," his friends say.

"The destination is where the Lord is taking us," he replies.

"But you must have some idea where that is, right?"

"No, I don't. We are counting on God to show us the way," Abraham says.

I love his honesty, and I think there is something to be gleaned here. Sometimes we think we know where we're going but in all honesty have no clue. Instead of pretending we know where life is taking us, wouldn't it be better to admit our uncertainty and ask God for direction? I have found that a God-directed adventure is always the best way, even when I am confused about which way.

Unexpected disappointment in Amsterdam led my travel partner and me to a new search in another direction. You may find yourself at a similar waypoint right now. Perhaps your bend in the road is due to the breakup of a relationship that is causing great sadness. Or maybe the troubling choices of someone you care about are causing tension in your family. You may be regretting some of your own choices that have taken you into unfamiliar territory. I hope you will see this is not the end of road even when you throw your backpack into the back seat of the wrong car and the driver has no idea where she is taking you.

No matter what part of this long and winding road you find yourself on, please know that God has not lost sight of you. It is normal to feel a bit mislead when life takes you in an unexpected direction, and your compass doesn't seem to be working. But even when you feel lost, God isn't. Direction will come as you follow God's promptings, and as you gain perspective by seeing where you've been through your rearview mirror.

And who knows—perhaps the detours of life are about finding a translator at the next oasis who will help you make sense out of a confusing set of circumstances. I remember being lost in the fjords of Alaska's Inside Passage desperate for guidance of any kind. More about that in the next chapter…

The Search for Meaning...

- What have you tried or acquired that failed to improve the value, quality or meaning of your life?
- Which of the following words best describes the road you're currently traveling? Smooth, bumpy, exhilarating, endless, dead end, off the beaten path, lost, hopeful. Explain.
- Think of a troubling situation from your past (perhaps involving a relationship). What have you learned from this experience as you reflect on it now?
- Write a paragraph about the direction or meaning you're looking for in life. What would you like from God at this point?

5 icy straight
Losing Your Way

The last evening of our Alaskan expedition came too quickly and I was determined not to waste a minute of it sitting around on our chartered live-aboard boat. I proposed to my friend Jim that we buzz over to a river we had previously visited using the eight-foot dingy we had on board. This would be our last chance to catch a salmon or spot a bear.

We studied a map showing the geographical irregularities of the area and judged we could reach the river in less than an hour. Jim was reluctant because it was getting late, but he decided to keep me company—a decision he soon regretted.

The small outboard raced along as we took mental notes of islands, channels, and rocky points for future reference. Finding the river was not difficult, and we celebrated our ability to navigate this part of Alaska's *Inside Passage* without our guide who we left behind on the mother boat. I snatched the fishing poles and Jim grabbed the rifle we carried for self-defense in case we encountered an aggressive bear. After two hours without catching a fish or spotting a bear, we both agreed it was time to hustle back to our home on the water.

But wait! The landmarks we counted on to guide us were no longer reliable. A huge incoming tide raised the water well over fifteen feet, altering the landscape. Small islands, inlets and rocky outcroppings were now buried under water. I slowed the motor to a troll while darting in and out of coves looking for the narrow passageway leading back to the yacht. Tide shifts in Alaska can be huge—a thirty foot rise or drop in tide levels is not uncommon.

Our choices were limited as night fell. We could continue to search the maze of inlets, but with decreasing visibility we risked puncturing our inflatable on a submerged rock. The other alternative was to venture off shore, following the five-mile-wide shipping lane called the *Icy Straight*. Without navigational lights and only a half tank of gas, we were taking a big risk—because we were very much lost.

As the dingy buzzed along at full throttle, we noticed a faint light on the black horizon. We jetted across the vast straight of water and found the light was coming from a working boat on the move. The diesel engine roared as we approached the large vessel from behind, and just crossing over the large swell it created was like sliding up and down a small hill. Could we approach this large vessel without being run over or capsized by its wake? And how would we get someone's attention over the noisy engine?

A few minutes later we noticed a crew member peering into the darkness through the fogged-up window of the cabin. It seemed unlikely that he'd stop for two guys in a rubber raft waving a gun at him! The ship steamed full speed ahead.

"Please help us!" we screamed. That worked!

The skipper opened the cabin door and yelled, "What in the #!/?# are you doing out here at this time of night in that skiff?" He then gave us a short but stern lecture on seamanship and safety, while questioning why our mothers gave birth to human beings the likes of us.

After we had been sufficiently humbled, he confirmed that our yacht was around a point marked by a light buoy visible in the distance. We thanked him and we went our separate ways like two ships, or a ship and a skiff in the night.

We motored around the point and were relieved to see our live-aboard anchored where we had left it several hours earlier. The skipper and our other buddies were on the deck with wine glasses in hand looking down at us like we were either the two luckiest numbskulls in the world or the most skilled seamen they'd ever seen. We claimed to be the latter and kept the real truth to ourselves.

• • • • •

I've often said, "Confession is good for the soul." And so I confess that I've learned the hard way to partner up with God in this adventure called *life*. What has gotten me into trouble time and again is my inclination to act impulsively, full speed ahead, come hell or high water. Worse yet, I am fully capable of charging forward without a thought as to whether God is providing direction or just along for the ride to see how long it takes for me to yell *help!* Call it built-in self confidence or flat out foolishness, I have a tendency to concoct plans without consulting God. This is a recipe for trouble.

Would you confess to a similar tendency? Do you typically try to figure out a course of action on your own, consulting God only if you find yourself in deep weeds? Or do you normally ask God for advice and guidance before you put a plan together? I admire you if you do the latter because that doesn't come naturally. Human beings are highly skilled when it comes to going off on our own and then asking God, "So how did this happen? Why am I in the mess I'm in? Where were you when I needed you?" God ends up taking the rap for all kinds of self-inflicted calamity.

Maybe this is why I love the disciple named Peter. Not only was he a fellow fisherman but he had an impetuous personality. One night he and his fishing pals were sailing across the Sea of Galilee. While straining to make headway against a stiff wind, they saw something that terrified them—what they thought was a ghost walking on the water. (Matthew 14:22-32)

Attempting to calm their fears, Jesus identified himself by saying, *"Take courage! It is I. Don't be afraid."* Though these words were meant to be comforting, they had to be bone-chilling too. This is when Peter came up with an idea that revealed either his reckless bravado or his bold faith. *"Lord, if it's you…tell me to come to you on the water."*

Have you lost your mind Peter? Remember where you are—in the middle of the Sea of Galilee in the darkness of night. I imagine all of his friends were thinking their buddy Peter was about to take a quantum leap off the deep end.

But not Jesus. *"Come,"* he said. And Peter did the unthinkable. *"Then Peter got down out of the boat, walked on the water and came toward Jesus,"* the Bible says. The disciples were surely slapping their heads in disbelief.

There was Peter, having the time of his life—until he started thinking he'd better get himself back on that boat. He was doing just fine until he had a mental lapse of who was in control of the situation. We read, *"But when he saw the wind, he was afraid and, beginning to sink, cried out, 'Lord save me!'"*

I have always considered this to be one of the greatest prayers ever prayed: "Lord save me!" Have you ever prayed this prayer? Many people like Peter have uttered these words in moments of desperation. But this can also be your prayer of faith as to who God is and what Jesus can do. I have had the privilege of listening to people ask God in prayer to save them from the cynicism of unbelief, from the shame of destructive behaviors, and from the despair of feeling unworthy or unloved. God loves to hear and respond to these kinds of prayers.

Where did Peter's plans go awry? He started out so well by consulting with Jesus about joining him on the water. He and God were together on this part of the plan. But the moment Peter took his mind off who was out there with him, he nearly drown. All he had to do was ask Jesus to guide him back to the boat and he'd have been just fine. Mercifully, Jesus responds to Peter's prayer by reaching down and saving him.

We point out how foolish Peter was, but I'm glad Jesus didn't do that. He simply asked, *"Why did you doubt?"* Good question. Why do we doubt? Why do we doubt God's ability to take us by the hand and lead us across unchartered waters? Why do we wonder if the journey Jesus has in mind could be superior to any venture we could dream up on our own? Why do we question whether God truly has our best interests in mind?

Thankfully, God knows we doubt because we are human. Thankfully, he is not shocked by our hesitations and concerns. When he hears our cries for mercy, he is right there to save us. It doesn't matter if we're impulsive or tentative by nature or something in between. God is there extending his hand to help us.

As I sat on the aft deck of the yacht witnessing a dazzling display of Northern Lights on our final night in Alaska, I was convicted by my natural inclination to overestimate my ability while underestimating God's. I gazed up at the orange and green shapes of the *Aurora Borealis* dancing across the sky and thought how ridiculous it is not to keep a tight grip on the hand of the One who created such stunning beauty. That night I expressed to God my desire to never venture into the unknown again without him directing my life's voyage. Perhaps you are ready to express to God a similar desire. Just remember, when you find yourself in trouble, pray that great prayer: *Lord, save me!*

Losing Your Way...

- Describe your personality in your own words. (Are you more of an introvert with contemplative traits or more of an extrovert with impulsive traits?)
- What would you say are the strengths and weaknesses of your personality?
- When do you normally ask God for guidance: before taking action, after taking action, on an as-needed basis, almost never. Explain.
- Think of a decision you must make or plan of action you are considering. I encourage you to take a moment and ask God to give you counsel and direction before moving forward.

6 night dives
Emerging from an Abyss

h ey John, we've got one more spot open on our lobster diving trip. Wanna go?" The question was posed by my buddy Dennis, the most fearless scuba diver I know. Spending three days on a live-aboard boat doing multiple dives around the Channel Islands was enough to whet my appetite. "Sure," I responded. "Count me in." I soon realized I should have asked more questions.

As the rookie among seventeen veteran lobster hunters on board, I felt intimidated. They portrayed a certain swagger, bantering back and forth about the lobsters they would catch. But most shocking was their blatant disregard for rule number one in diving—always dive with a partner.

After completing five separate dives on the first day, I had yet to see a lobster, much less capture one. That was about to change when darkness fell. As we were suiting up Dennis said, "Well John, since this is your first night dive, I will be your partner."

"That's what you said before our first dive this morning," I replied. "I gave up trying to keep pace with you—it was like you had a propeller attached to your backside."

"Tonight will be different—I promise," Dennis said with that wry smile of his. His promise was not reassuring. The thought of diving alone at night gave me the willies. I grabbed a spare dive light and made sure my compass was reading correctly.

The two of us plunged off the deck of the sixty-five foot dive boat and floated to the surface to make sure all of our equipment functioned properly. The bright floodlight beaming from the upper deck reassured me. Little did I know then how much it would mean in the hour ahead.

We wove our way through a thick kelp forest, a kind of underwater maze of overgrown vegetation. The ocean forest looked haunted as our lights created streaks of illumination that bounced off the kelp stalks. We were swimming toward shore where the vegetation gave way to exposed rock piles where spiny back lobsters love to hide.

These night-loving creatures will emerge from their secret daytime haunts and crawl into the open under cover of darkness. But no sooner had we begun looking for lobsters than I found myself looking for Dennis. Where did he go? I did a complete "360" with my light shining in all directions but I couldn't see him. Putting my training to use, I stayed put, hoping he'd return. But after a few minutes of wasting precious air, it appeared he had abandoned me.

Now what do I do? I visualized everything from sharks to sea monsters emerging out of the watery blackness. I had to get a grip on myself or I'd be in serious trouble. Panic is by far the worst enemy that any diver faces.

I realized I had two alternatives. Swim back to the ship by relying on my compass to reverse my course, or continue searching for lobster. I decided on the second plan. But first I made a slow ascent from the bottom to the surface to see if I could get a physical reference point.

I stuck my head out of the water and saw the most glorious thing—the light of our ship beaming some two hundred yards in the distance! There was home base. There was safety. As I gazed at that light, fear melted away.

I double checked my compass and verified the direction back to the boat was correct. I let the air out of my vest and began sinking to the bottom again, realizing my biggest fear was not sharks or sea monsters. My biggest fear was being underwater in complete darkness—alone.

· · · · ·

Being alone, or just feeling alone is one of the biggest monsters any of us face. And so we do our best to stay connected with friends, hang out with buddies and share life with trusted partners. But we also know what it's like when our friends are not available, when our buddies are nowhere to be found, and when our trusted partners abandon us.

In truth, we live life alone. We are alone with our thoughts, feelings and experiences. At times we may feel misunderstood, overlooked or neglected. Ironically, feelings of isolation may creep in even when surrounded by a sea of people.

A hard truth about life is that all human relationships are temporary. Separation by distance, divorce, disagreement, desertion or death is a sad reality and none of us is immune.

So what can we do when we're alone in the darkness? Personal experience has proven to me that nothing is more reassuring than turning to God—not as a last resort but as the first one. God serves as our guiding light, trustworthy compass, and reassuring presence that never abandons or gives up on us.

A story in the Gospel of Mark about Jesus' disciples in their boat one night illustrates this truth (Mark 4:35-41). Jesus was with them catching up on sleep. But while they were sailing towards the other side of the Sea of Galilee, a furious squall came up. The waves crashed over the side of the boat and the men panicked. So they yelled to Jesus, *"Teacher, don't you care if we drown?"*

Fear kept them from seeing reality. Of course Jesus cared about their situation. After all, he was in the boat with them! They were not alone. God was there. But they failed to recognize this reality.

But what opened their eyes to the powerful presence with them were a few words spoken by Jesus: *"Quiet! Be still!"* With that simple command, the wind and the waves died down and the sea became as calm as a frog pond. Jesus then asked his friends a simple question: *"Why are you so afraid? Do you still have no faith?"* God had not abandoned them. He had been with them the entire time. Jesus was simply asking them to trust.

Sometimes it's hard to be aware of God's presence when you're alone—or feel alone—even more so when you're in a panic and there's no one in sight. I know the feeling well. But we can emerge from that dark and lonely abyss, pop our heads above the surface and see that guiding light. God is always there—you can count on that.

Once I saw the light of the dive boat and began hunting again, I saw lobsters! All day long I had seen nothing. That night I captured my first one, then my second, then my third, fourth, fifth and sixth. I was elated. In a matter of minutes, this night had been transformed from total desperation to sheer jubilation.

I returned to the boat and ripped off my wet suit off before Dennis climbed on board. He gave me that familiar smile as if to say, *What happened to you? Can't understand how we got separated again.* I was about to make a sarcastic comment about his leaving me in the lurch when I noticed his empty lobster bag.

"Buddy ol' friend," I said, "how many lobsters did you find after you ditched me?"

"I came up empty. How about you?"

I gave him a smile of my own and said, "My bag is in the live well. You can take a look for yourself."

I watched his jaw drop open as he peered into my sack and saw the half dozen beautiful spiny backs flipping around. "Maybe if you'd stick with me I could show you a thing or two about where to find those bad boys." I laughed. He didn't.

That night I lay in my bunk reflecting on the adventures of the day as a gentle swell rocked the boat. What struck me most was that God had been little more than an afterthought as I went about my activities that day. I was focused on the next dive, the next hunt, everything else but God. Even when I was alone in the dark, my God-awareness was pretty weak. And so I spent some time in my bunk reconnecting with him. I prayed and asked God to swim with me the next day, and to stay by my side when I lost sight of my partner. He did, and not once did I feel alone after that prayer. What a difference to sense that God was below the surface with me.

Perhaps you find yourself alone right now and would be willing to pray a simple prayer to God. If you can, take a moment to acknowledge his presence with you. You might ask him to be your guiding light or a strong presence when up against powerful currents. If you feel lead, ask God to show you how to build a more vital connection with him. This could be the start of something very special between you and God—being the One you count on when no one else is there.

Emerging from an Abyss...

- Think of a time when someone abandoned you and you felt alone. How did you react or what did you do in that situation?
- Identify a situation when a perceived threat caused you to panic. Did the danger turn out to be real, potential or imaginary?
- How often in your day-to-day living do you think about God being present with you: almost never, sometimes, or almost always. What could you do that would help you be more aware of God's presence?
- Consider taking Jesus' words to the turbulent sea as words directed to you: "Quiet! Be still!" Take a few moments to be quiet and still, and practice being present with God who is present with you.

7 the orphan
Alone on the Street

t he small cardboard box sat on the sidewalk next to the curb of this impoverished neighborhood in Quito, Ecuador. My wife Debbie and I were visiting friends in this area en route to a missionary assignment in Argentina. The street was conspicuously empty. We were curious about this abandoned container. We slowed our pace and peeked over the tattered edge.

What we saw stopped us in our tracks. Inside that box was a living, breathing baby girl wrapped in a soiled blanket. We glanced at each other in disbelief. What was this child doing alone on the street? Where was her mother? We scanned our surroundings thinking her family must not be far away. But there was no one.

We reached down and pulled the pink blanket back just enough to see her pretty round face and her jet black hair. She slept peacefully. Our hearts went out to her. What, if anything, could we do?

We considered taking her with us, but that was impossible. We couldn't just walk off with a child who wasn't ours. That would get us into trouble for sure. And we had a curious feeling that someone might be watching and waiting to take advantage of a foolish move on our part. Sadly, we walked away, praying that somehow this child would be rescued and cared for by someone.

Like most all people that we met in South America, the Ecuadorian people are kind, generous and uphold high family values. But like many places in the world, poverty makes it difficult for parents to provide for their children. In the absence of other known alternatives, the sad reality is that newborns sometimes become orphans on the street. But that scene haunted us for months afterward, often wondering what ever happened to that precious child.

Fast-forward to one year later when we were on our way home from Argentina. During a layover at the Miami airport, we bumped into the son and daughter-in-law of missionaries whom we had worked with in South America. We embraced each other and expressed amazement at what appeared to be a remarkable coincidence.

But we knew this was no fluke when our friends told us why they were in the Miami airport. Their newly adopted child was on an incoming flight—from Quito, Ecuador! We were speechless as our thoughts turned to the orphan in the cardboard box from a year earlier.

We were as giddy as the parents as we watched the plane arrive and the agent emerge with a baby in her arms. What joy to witness the parents embrace their precious child wrapped in pink. It was a girl, with a pretty round face and jet black hair. No longer orphaned, she now had a new family and a new identity that would change her life forever.

Our tears flowed as we flew home from that trip. How stark the contrast between the sadness of a child abandoned and the joy of a child adopted. Debbie and I thanked God for orchestrating this unexpected event in a way that put bookends around our entire year abroad. We had seen so much brokenness in our world—it was good to see something healed.

· · · · ·

The plight of an orphan was hard for me to grasp until I read the Bible. Scripture opened my eyes to a clear truth—that all of us are in need of adoption. Like you, I have biological parents who conceived and named me. But there is another Parent—God the Father—who yearns to adopt us into his family. While God wants to "pick us up off the street," we must give him our consent by agreeing to be his spiritual daughter or son. No one is born into the Family of God—adoption is the only way in. The following is an example of how the Bible speaks of spiritual adoption: *"Praise be to the God and Father of our Lord Jesus Christ...In love he predestined us for adoption to sonship through Jesus Christ, in accordance with his pleasure and will..."* (Ephesians 1:3, 5)

The writer uses the word "sonship" as a reference to the full legal standing of an adopted male heir under first century Roman law. In the same way, the Father-God wants us, chooses us, even plans for us to be his adopted children. God sent his only non-adopted Son, Jesus Christ, to reveal how much his Father loves us and longs for us to be part of his family. But as much as our heavenly Father wants us to be his kids, we must choose to accept him as our Father. With God as our Father, we become members of a global family as the Bible declares:

"Consequently, you are no longer foreigners and strangers, but fellow citizens with God's people and also members of his household…" (Ephesians 2:19)

The words "foreigners" and "strangers" describe our situation as orphans without a spiritual home. But as members of our Father's household, we inherit a new identity as brothers and sisters in the Family of God. My favorite picture of this grand blended family is the Apostle Paul praying to God the Father in this way: *"…I kneel before the Father, from whom every family in heaven and on earth derives its name."* (Ephesians 3:14, 15)

This statement is such good news, especially for those who come from a broken home or didn't have a father or mother's love. The Family of God can be the family you never had. Many experience family love for the first time in their lives by connecting with a church family. Like any family, churches consist of imperfect members. But this is also where we can find caring sisters and brothers who can help fill the void and heal the hurt of feeling orphaned.

Perhaps you're having difficulty accepting God as your Father because your earthly father abandoned or abused you. Please know that God understands your struggle to come to him. Even in the struggle, the Father in heaven continues to choose you, hope for you, and plans for you to come home. God can become the loving Father you never knew.

On a personal note, adoption has taken on special meaning to Debbie and me as our son and daughter-in-law, Aaron and Gretchen, have been trying to adopt a child. Twice they've gone through the process of having birth moms choose them to be the parents of their babies. And both times have ended in heartbreaking outcomes when the father of each child turned up and reclaimed them. Voicing no objection during the entire adoption process, both fathers went against the desires of the mothers, causing great distress for all involved.

Perhaps you have lost a child and understand the gut-wrenching angst that Aaron and Gretchen have been through. As difficult as this is, we have to believe that this is not the end of your story—that our Father God has something surprising in store for you. In our son and daughter-in-law's case, one month before losing the second child—a little girl, Gretchen found out she was pregnant! What a wonderful and unexpected development for them.

At the same time, she and Aaron found themselves in a perplexing situation. Their pregnancy came while they were still mourning the loss of their adopted baby girl. In spite of those mixed emotions, joy overcame sorrow when little Logan was born. Less than two years later, joy was multiplied by the birth of their second child, a girl named Reese. Through this unpredictable journey, God has sustained them, guided them, and drawn them closer together.

Aaron and Gretchen still have it in their hearts to adopt, and are now working with an agency representing the country of Ethiopia. I remember something Gretchen said about this process: "Even though our Ethiopian daughter is yet to be identified, we are waiting for her, longing for her, already believing she is ours even though she is not home yet."

That is exactly how God sees us. He waits for us, longs for us, choosing to believe we are his even though we are not home yet. And the day we decide to run into his waiting arms is the day we discover our new identity as children of an eternal Father. This is also the day we'll find ourselves celebrating with other orphans who are no longer alone, but who have found a home in the Family of God.

Alone on the Street...

- While you were growing up, was your family healthy, unhealthy, or somewhere in between? Explain.
- Are you currently close or distant with your family members? Explain.
- What comes to mind when you think about adoption? Does being adopted have special meaning to you or to someone you know? Explain.
- What do you find appealing, if anything, about being a son or daughter in God's Family?
- If you haven't asked God to be your adoptive Father, would you consider doing that now? Perhaps you can express this in a simple prayer.

8 killer bees
Surviving an Attack

Six of us stepped off the commercial airplane in Manaus, Brazil and took our first breath of the steamy tropical air. We stood about 1,000 miles upriver from where the Amazon River empties into the Atlantic Ocean. But this would not be our last stop. The pilot of a small plane was ready to fly us another two hours over the roadless jungle to our fishing lodge.

Looking down, we saw nothing but a solid carpet of lush greenery appearing between the foggy mist over the rain forest. As we began descending, a narrow dirt strip cut out of the jungle came into view giving new meaning to the phrase *in the middle of nowhere.*

The friendly Brazilian staff escorted us to our rooms built on the banks of the river. The following day we'd pursue a spectacular sport fish known as the "Peacock Bass." When hooked, these large rainbow-colored fish would fight like finned maniacs on steroids. But other creatures of a much smaller variety also commanded our attention.

The locals spoke of poisonous snakes, venomous frogs and deadly spiders. We were also warned to keep an eye out for killer bees. These aggressive insects, a type of hybrid honeybee, are known to swarm a fleeing victim while stinging him relentlessly. One night some of the guys got firsthand experience with these nasty insects on a boat tour of the river.

The guides encouraged us to go out after dark in order to view critters rarely seen in the light of day. After hearing about all the things that could kill us, it took some convincing before we agreed—and then with some reluctance! Once in the boats, the guides scanned the shorelines with their powerful searchlights. We were amazed at how these native Brazilians could see the glow of tiny eyeballs long before we spotted them. As we trolled along they would point to a spot on shore and say *frog* or *snake* or *gator.*

We ventured out in two groups, and when our buddies in the other boat returned to the lodge they couldn't wait to tell our group what happened to them. The excitement started when their guide spotted a small crocodile on the muddy bank of the river. He maneuvered the boat into the small bay where the croc was resting. The light seemed to mesmerize the animal, allowing the boat came to rest within a few feet of him.

The guide then handed the searchlight to one of the guys in the boat. His job was to shine the light on the croc as the guide quietly slipped over the side. My buddies watched in disbelief as the man waded in the shallow water toward the motionless reptile. With the animal now at his feet, he quickly reached down and grabbed him behind the head with one hand and behind the back legs with his other hand. Once he had a firm grip on the writhing creature, he picked it up and thrust the croc over his head in a gesture of victory. Then all hell broke loose.

Of all the bad luck, he hit a bee's nest in the branches of a tree overhead. The guys in the boat watched the horror scene unfold as a cloud of angry bees flew out of the nest and attacked their intruder. The guide threw the gator down and ran out into deeper water, but the bees followed and stung him repeatedly.

Meanwhile there was pandemonium in the boat as the bees descended on my friends who ducked down and covered themselves as best they could. They could hear the guide screaming words in Portuguese, but the only thing the Americans could understand was, "Dios mio! Dios mio!" meaning, *My God! My God!*

The guide kept barking unintelligible words. Finally one of the guys realized what he meant. "I think he wants us to turn out the light." That made sense since the bees were attracted to whatever was illuminated, enabling them to see their target. Someone switched off light and in the pitch dark the men listened to the eerie sounds of the bees buzzing and the guide moaning.

Slowly the guide felt his way toward the boat and climbed over the side. He started the motor, backed out quickly and then raced away from the scene. Only when they were a safe distance from the danger zone did he slow down, stop the motor, and turn on the light. He took off his shirt revealing dozens of red welts on his back, shoulders, arms, and neck. The multiple bites did not kill him but he was a very sick man for the next several days.

• • • • •

As I listened to the numerous comments about this unnerving adventure, the word *humbling,* expressed by one of my friends, stood out. "I will never forget cowering under rain jackets with a group of grown men who were rendered defenseless by insects.

That was a humbling experience," he said. "It was a vivid reminder of how vulnerable we are despite our outward bravado. My manly pride took a hit tonight."

I complimented him. It was refreshing to hear a man speak of personal humility in a transparent manner. Pride commonly prevents us from admitting our weaknesses, cowardice, or giving any indication that we're not strong enough to handle what life throws at us. Because of the competitive nature of our culture, we are trained not to reveal personal vulnerability. We want our competitors to think there are no chinks in our armor. But we know that this is a facade. Weakness and struggle are inherently human. Trying to prop up an image of invincibility is an exhausting chore and eventually becomes impossible to maintain.

I've heard people say they could never pray to God until they improved their behavior and cleaned up their act. They believe their less than admirable lifestyles have offended God and render their prayers useless. But I've found that transparency combined with humility is exactly what God wants from us. He already knows our faults and limitations. What grabs his attention is when we own up to our flaws and are honest about our inadequacies.

Appropriate humility is a safeguard against the pretentious idea that we can do better or get better on our own. A humble spirit prevents us from thinking that we can handle the inevitable crisis without God's help. As we grow accustomed to confessing our weaknesses and struggles, we'll find that God responds with compassion and grace. A parable in Luke's Gospel is a good example of authentic humility:

To some who were confident of their own righteousness and looked down on everyone else, Jesus told this parable: "Two men went up to the temple to pray, one a Pharisee and the

*other a tax collector. The Pharisee stood by himself and prayed:
'God, I thank you that I am not like other people—robbers,
evildoers, adulterers—or even like this tax collector. I fast
twice a week and give a tenth of all I get.'*

*"But the tax collector stood at a distance. He would not
even look up to heaven, but beat his breast and said, 'God,
have mercy on me, a sinner.'*

*"I tell you that this man, rather than the other, went
home justified before God. For all those who exalt themselves
will be humbled, and those who humble themselves will be
exalted."* (Luke 18:9-14)

Sometimes religion can do strange things to people, like
making them think they're superior to others. Jesus sets the
record straight by saying that true religion has nothing to do
with one flawed human being comparing himself with another.
Nor does true religion have anything to do with acts of piety
designed to impress God or to earn his favor. Jesus makes it
clear that true religion is having a heart that seeks after God and
yearns for his mercy.

God smiles when we are transparent about who we are and
what we need. God's favor rests upon those humble enough to
admit their inability to impress him with their performance.
Acknowledging that we are sinners is being authentic about what
we know about ourselves and what God knows about us. A humble
spirit reminds us that there is a God and we are not him.

Living life is so much better when we take ourselves less
seriously and God more seriously. God is not looking for greater
self-confidence or a better track record before we turn to him.
Rather, he is looking for an authentic person who says, "Here I am
Lord. I'm not pretty, but I need you very much in my life." You

can be sure God receives that prayer with joy, and will release you from the tiring task of trying to be someone you're not.

Dios mio! Dios mio! is also an effective prayer. My wife and I found ourselves praying a similar prayer while held up at gunpoint in Argentina one evening. More about that in the next chapter…

Surviving an Attack…

- Think of a time in your life when pride caused you to react in a regretful way. What did you learn, if anything, about yourself?
- Define humility in your own words. In what way do you think the concept of humility might be misunderstood in society today?
- What do you think it means to be honest with God? How different would your prayers be if you were transparent with God about your life?
- Consider praying what is sometimes called "The Sinner's Prayer" by repeating it slowly several times in a row. Pause a moment before repeating it each time, sincerely and thoughtfully: *"God, have mercy on me, a sinner."*

9

ak-47's
Dodging a Bullet

Without warning, a tranquil summer evening turned chaotic. Our church service had just concluded when two military trucks raced up and screeched to a halt. Soldiers dressed in camo fatigues jumped out of the trucks, hustling toward us. They weren't there to worship. That was obvious!

With *AK-47's* in ready position, one of the soldiers yelled, "Line up against the wall— everybody!" The twenty of us glanced at each other with a wince and a frown. My heart was pounding as we walked toward the exterior wall of the church. Many were mumbling their prayers.

Nobody had any idea what this was about. Had someone committed a crime? Were they looking for the perpetrators? Were we worshipping too loudly that night? Had the neighbors complained? Who or what were they looking for? I was hoping it wasn't me—or my wife who had the look of terror in her eyes.

The place was Argentina. The year was 1976. The military dictatorship of the Juan Peron era had an iron grip on the country. A no-nonsense militaristic presence overshadowed every city and province. Anyone considered a threat or suspected of opposing the existing regime was apprehended. People often disappeared, never to be heard from again. These possibilities raced through my mind as we stood in line.

"Documentes! Pasaportes!" barked one of the soldiers. We were required to carry identification at all times. Problem was, I didn't have my passport with me.

One by one, the soldiers checked the documents of the local people in the line-up. Closer and closer they got to where I was standing. My wife Debbie, being the responsible person she is, had her passport in hand. But I, being the let's not worry about such things person, realized I should have listened to her!

Of course, we could have avoided this whole scene had we stayed in our hometown where everything was routine and safe. But after two years of seminary and two years of marriage, I sensed a need to discover more about who I was as a person, more about who we were as a couple, and more about what we were supposed to do with the rest of our lives.

That is when we heard about a one-year missionary assignment in Argentina. This opportunity seemed to have our names written all over it since I was sensing a strong pull to do mission work in the third world. As we began to say *yes* to this endeavor, we soon found ourselves on a God-directed adventure that served to shape the course of our lives.

However, I wasn't particularly sensing God's direction when a soldier with a big gun approached my wife and said, "Pasaporte Senora!" I wasn't scared for her. I was scared for myself!

I still hadn't thought of anything to say. My mind went blank. My mouth went dry. I broke out in a cold sweat. When he looked at me and said, "Pasaporte Senior!" I blurted out the first words that entered my head. "I belong to her!" I said, pointing to my wife.

Crazy as it was, that answer seemed to satisfy him. We were the only two white people in the lineup besides the resident missionary couple. I guess he figured we belonged to each other. It was one of the times I was very thankful for holy matrimony—and for a spouse who stood with me when the chips were down.

Debbie and I discovered a lot about ourselves that year in South America. We realized cross-cultural work in the third world was not what we were wired to do in the long term. We learned that love in a marriage is a courageous commitment, not just a sentimental feeling. And we found out God is very much present, even when staring down the barrel of a gun.

• • • • •

Our experience in Argentina required us to address a common misconception about the Christian life. Perhaps you've heard a Christian say something like this: *If you commit your life to Christ and maintain a strong faith, God will protect you from the trials and difficulties other people face.* The implication is that the moment you stop excluding God and start seeking him, your life will be trouble-free. Sometimes this is expressed to persuade someone to profess Jesus as their Savior. This is unfortunate because this view doesn't reflect the truth.

God never promised that a Christian would be shielded from the challenges a non-Christian will encounter. The Bible nowhere states that accepting Jesus into your life guarantees protection from the evils of this world. If we are confused about this, we need to remember what happened to Jesus. He lived a perfect life and was crucified for it!

Not only that, let's consider what Jesus said to his devoted followers. He encouraged them to trust him for their daily needs, and told them not to worry. *"Therefore do not worry about tomorrow, for tomorrow will worry about itself."* Then he added, *"Each day has enough trouble of its own."* (Matthew 6:34)

Wouldn't we agree? Jesus declares that the adventure called *life* includes more than its share of trouble. We don't have to go looking for problems—they will surely seek us out. Trouble is rather indiscriminate as to who it finds.

Not long before Jesus was apprehended and killed by his enemies, he explained to his disciples that his death and resurrection were part of God's plan. He urged them not to worry about what was about to happen—then blessed them with his peace. "I have told you these things, so that in me you may have peace." Then he stated, *"In this world you will have trouble. But take heart! I have overcome the world."* (John 16:33)

Jesus makes it clear that while there are few guarantees in this life, trouble is one of them. While we may find little comfort in this reality, at least we can't say we haven't been warned. Consider this—if it's true that God makes life easier for people of faith, then why did two missionaries doing their best to serve God get held up at gunpoint outside of a church, causing my young wife to question why she ever said *I do* to me?

I had some questions of my own after I found out the soldiers who held us up that night were just out having some fun. I'm not kidding! Word on the street the next day was that these young men were facing a common problem in the military—boredom. They decided that putting a little scare into the Christians would be entertaining on an otherwise uneventful Sunday evening.

Naturally this caused me to ask, *God, what is that about? You are supposed to be on our side, looking out for us, right? Here we are doing your work, trying to help these impoverished people down here, and this is what we get for it? This is not what we signed up for! Why don't you send those bored soldiers after some real troublemakers instead of harassing us Christians?*

What was God's answer to this? Well as I quit complaining and started reading, I found Jesus saying this about our Father-God: *"He causes his sun to rise on the evil and the good, and sends rain on the righteous and the unrighteous."* (Matthew 5:45b) The warmth of the sun falls on the faces of all human beings without distinction. Life-giving rain falls on those who do right and on those who do wrong. God sends what is delightful and dreadful without favoritism. Pleasure and pain are an inseparable part of the package called life.

This isn't to say that seeking to live a God-honoring life doesn't have its advantages—it most certainly does. Choosing a God-directed course will help you avoid many of the pitfalls that going down a self-directed path can lead to. A vital connection with God also provides a great source of resilience when the going gets rough. What's more, partnering with God can bolster your courage when fear has you on your heels. As you strengthen your relationship with him, see if God doesn't give you an extra degree of toughness, an extra measure of tenacity, an extra level of resolve to keep you going when you are up against a wall.

Inviting God to have more influence in your life has another potential benefit. You may notice yourself thinking fewer of those self-absorbed, *woe is me* kind of thoughts. When you're inclined to feel sorry for yourself, see if God doesn't have a way of pulling you out of defeatist thinking. I have found it's harder to have a pity party with God whispering truth into my ears.

You may even find yourself taking the question, *"What did I do to deserve this?"* and turn it on its head. You will ask that question not because you're having a bad time, but because you're having the time of your life! More about that in the next chapter...

Dodging a Bullet...

- Think of a time when you thought, *"What did I do to deserve this?"* What was going on?
- Describe a situation when you were not spared trouble even though you asked for God's protection. What kind of disappointment, if any, did you express to God?
- If you are a person who desires to live a more God-directed life, name some benefits you have discovered, if any, along the way.
- What is the biggest surprise, question, challenge or discovery you have made so far as you strengthen your relationship with God?

10   helicopter drops
When Heaven Meets Earth

t he helicopter trembled as the rotor blades lifted our small band of skiers off the snow-covered landing pad. Ascending from the 6,000-foot level, we climbed above the trees to over 10,000 feet. Mountain peaks and valleys blanketed in white lay before us as far as the eye could see.

We were about to be off-loaded onto a desolate peak somewhere in the Canadian Rockies and our bodies shook with adrenaline. Through our headsets we listened to the pilot and guide chatter about which ridge-top would be safe enough to land the chopper. My fellow skiers and I looked at each other as if to say: "What have we gotten ourselves into?"

Skiing with the aid of a helicopter is the *Holy Grail* for snow skiers and something I thought I would never do. But one day a friend made me an offer I couldn't refuse: "Hey John, my son and

I planned to hook up with some friends of mine for a helicopter skiing trip. But my son has college exams that week, so I'm wondering if you'd like to take his place."

"Seriously?" I asked. "Give me two seconds to think this over…Yes! Count me in!"

The eight of us met on the tarmac of a small local airport where we boarded a private jet owned by one of my buddy's friends. On our flight to Canada, I learned my new skiing partners were both highly skilled professionals and highly experienced partiers. As the drinks started flowing, I also learned that none of them had darkened the door of a church for a long, long time.

Landing in Vancouver, a member of the Royal Canadian Mounted Police approached our plane. Charlie, the owner of the jet, leaned over to me, "John, watch and learn."

The officer boarded and welcomed us to British Columbia. He then asked three simple questions. "What will you be doing in Canada?"

"Skiing," Charlie answered.

"And how long will you be staying?" was the second question.

"One week."

The third question is where I would *watch and learn.*" "Do you have any firearms, drugs or alcohol on board?" the officer asked.

"No."

"Well then, enjoy your visit to our country." With that the officer exited the plane.

Once he was out of sight, the guys unload several cases of high-end wine and booze stashed in the cargo compartment. I could just imagine the headlines in my hometown newspaper: *Local Pastor Held in Canadian Jail for Smuggling Alcohol Across the Border.*

From Vancouver, two helicopters whisked us away through mountain passes to our ski lodge. The next day we hovered over a mountain peak as the pilot barked on the intercom: "DO NOT GO TOWARD THE FRONT OF THE CHOPPER WHEN YOU GET OUT—GO TOWARD THE BACK! IF YOU GO TOWARD THE FRONT YOU WILL DROP OUT OF SIGHT INTO A 2000-FOOT VERTICAL CREVASSE AND WE WILL NEVER SEE YOU AGAIN! AM I MAKING MYSELF CLEAR?" No one needed further clarification. We were all about to pee our pants.

We touched down on what seemed like the top of the world. Skiers and equipment were off-loaded and the guide gave the all-clear signal to the pilot. We watched the helicopter disappear over a distant ridge and stood in awe of the endless ridge tops, chutes, bowls, and walls of white surrounding us. We had arrived in skier heaven.

Six giddy snow-hounds began carving figure-eights through the light virgin powder. Snorkels may have been helpful as the waist-deep snow flew into our faces and over our heads. From top to bottom, from peak to peak, from dawn to dusk, from one trackless wall of snow to another we skied till our legs turned to rubber and darkness fell.

• • • • •

Skiing the equivalent of Mount Everest in vertical feet was more than enough excitement for one day. But I remembered those cases of wine, and knew going to bed early was not going to happen. Predictably, the evenings turned into excess as the partying commenced and copious amounts of expensive California cabernet were poured and consumed.

Being part of a scene like this may seem incongruous for a person on a quest to live a God-honoring life. Wisdom might tell us to avoid influences that could weaken rather than strengthen our relationship with God. And each of us must be discerning about this. But as we are able, God calls us to engage with people on their turf instead of isolating ourselves from them.

Think about the twelve disciples, the men Jesus spent the most time with during his three-year ministry. Who were these guys? Four were fishermen, one a tax collector, one a member of a radical political party, and the other six we know practically nothing about. And there were no religious leaders among them— not a Bible scholar or Sunday School teacher in the group.

Where did Jesus find these guys? On their turf along the seashore, at the tax collector's office, in their homes, and at their feasts and parties. And during his ministry, Jesus often made a point of engaging with people who were avoided by others— people like prostitutes and the demon possessed.

Shortly before Jesus' death he prayed for his friends and followers. He said this to his Father in heaven: *"My prayer is not that you take them out of the world but that you protect them from the evil one...As you sent me into the world, I have sent them into the world."* (John 17:15, 18)

A Christ-follower is called to be in the world where people who need God live and work and play. This is not an easy assignment, but Jesus promises us his protection and wisdom in situations where it would be easy to compromise our convictions. This is where we can be *in* the world, but not *of* it. The people Christ wants us to influence are not just those found inside the walls of a church. Sometimes we find ourselves in unexpected environments because God wants us there.

I have found that being present is the most important thing I do in a party setting. I avoid being judgmental about what people are doing or saying. But I also come with personal boundaries already established when it comes to drinking, drugs, and other behaviors. Generally people respect that. Beyond this, I wait for opportunities to be an influence.

Consider what happened during those all-night parties in Canada. In the middle of what seemed like a hopeless and irredeemable scene, something surprising took place. The men lowered their personal guard, they laid their pretense aside, and suddenly it didn't matter that a religious guy was among them. Without my prompting, subjects concerning God and spirituality came up naturally.

"I'm an atheist," one of them said to me. "Tell me why you're not."

Another chimed in, "If God is a God of love, why is there so much suffering and injustice in the world?"

Later someone asked, "What about all the scientific evidence that supports evolution and contradicts a creationist point of view?"

The questions and discussions continued long into the night.

Theoretical or philosophical questions often get more personal as trust builds. Later in the week, one of the guys started sharing the problems in his marriage. Another wanted to talk about the breakdown in communication with his daughter. He expressed regret about not providing a better spiritual foundation for his kids and wondered if it was too late to start. I assured him it was not.

The cool thing is that these spiritual conversations did not start and end in Canada. This was the beginning of a journey with a couple of the men. One was the owner of the jet, and the other was the biggest knock-down-drag-out partier of the whole bunch. Both of these buddies agreed to be part of a small group, and while it took several months for one, and a couple of years for the other, both of them came to embrace Christ as their Lord and Savior. Best of all, they are now influencing their friends to do the same.

Please do not think you need to be a long-time Christian to be a spiritual influence in someone's life. As a matter of fact, I have observed that spiritual explorers and beginners in the faith are often the best at this because they have so many friends who are on a similar level. Being an influence for God in someone else's life can lead to some of the most incredible adventures ever.

That said, none of our efforts to live Christ's life or reflect his life to others will be effective without God's grace. We all need massive doses of grace all the time—something I learned in an encounter with Clint Eastwood one day. More about that in the next chapter…

When Heaven Meets Earth…

- What was the most extreme thing you ever did?
- Identify a social setting where the actions of others were making you uncomfortable. What did you do?
- What hobbies, activities or interests, if any, give you the opportunity to form friendships with people who are non-Christians?
- Think about a conversation you may have had about God with a non-religious friend. What did you talk about?

11 clint eastwood
Grabbing Hold of Grace

e verything about Clint Eastwood says 'tough guy.' In most of his movie roles, he looks tough, talks tough, and acts tough. Perhaps the phrase, *Go ahead, make my day!* personifies his career more than any other. When Clint Eastwood looks you in the eye, you know he means business.

Mr. Eastwood has another passion besides making movies. He loves to play golf, and has designed his own private course in the hills of Monterey, California. If you buy a hat in the pro shop, the name *Tehama* appears on the front, and on the back are the Latin words, *Fac Diem Meam*—meaning *Make My Day*. Clint Eastwood is a tough guy, even on the golf course.

I've had the privilege of playing his course several times as part of a small pastors' retreat each January. One day my golfing partners and I were sufficiently humbled by our level of play and frustration was mounting. As our foursome stepped up to the twelfth tee with drivers in hand, we saw two guys sauntering along the left side of the fairway about 200 yards away. We had to wait for them to move on as they were well within striking range.

I think God was teaching me a lesson in patience that day, but sometimes I'm a slow learner. I shouted in a voice that may have been heard 200 yards away, "I wish these guys would hurry up and get off *our* golf course!"

Once I had made this moronic statement, I proceeded to yell *"FORE!"* in order to get their attention. And I did. These two clueless people who were holding up our play looked back at us. That was all we needed to safely tee off, and that is exactly what we did.

Whoosh! Whoosh! Whoosh! Whoosh! All four of us drove our balls over the heads of the two guys now patiently waiting for us. After we had finished, they turned and continued strolling up the fairway.

We returned to our golf carts and my partner turned to me. "Hey John, look at how that guy walks."

"Yeah, so?" I started driving the cart down the fairway.

"Slow down, man," my friend said. "Look at the gait of the guy on the left. Doesn't he look familiar?"

I took a closer look at the slender guy with the grayish hair strolling along, and then it hit me. "No! Can't be! Is it really?"

"Sure is. We just hit all four of our golf balls over Clint Eastwood's head!" my buddy said.

"I can't believe this! And I had the nerve to ask what this clueless guy was doing on *our* golf course!"

I then slowed the golf cart to a crawl. "There's no way I'm going to drive by him. Let's wait till he walks past the green." I was thinking that if we got any closer he might pull out his .44 and say, *Go ahead, make my day!*

At the end of our round, we asked the guys in the pro shop if Mr. Eastwood was out on the course that day. Sure enough, they confirmed he was with the course manager checking on maintenance issues. We asked if he mentioned anything that happened on the twelfth fairway. "No. No problems," they said. I was relieved.

I know I'll never live this down, and also know that my fellow pastors have mercilessly embellished this story at my expense. Some have used it in sermons at their churches, telling about the pastor of CrossWinds Church who impatiently confronted Clint Eastwood, told him to get off his own golf course, hit golf balls at him, and did not act like Jesus at all—and so on. I guess I had it coming.

• • • • •

You may be thinking that as a pastor I should know better and behave better than I did. I'm willing to admit that despite my efforts, I often fall short of being the person I want to be. I try to practice what I preach, seek the counsel of others, read my Bible, pray for God's help, and I've read countless books about how to create a new and improved me. Maybe you've done the same for yourself. While much of this is helpful, I've found there is no comprehensive fix that will transform us into people of unblemished character. So what is a person to do?

Is it simply a matter of trying harder? Many religious systems, in fact, are built on this foundation. The goal is to earn God's favor and thus get to heaven someday. So you follow the rules, practice the codes of conducts, obey the commandments, do good, be good, and if that's not working, at least try to look good.

But what if we don't live up to expectations? What if we don't perform as required? That's when guilt can work its magic, providing ample motivation to keep us trying harder, ever hopeful to turn God's frown into a smile.

On the other hand, what if we think we're performing pretty well, and guilt is not our problem? This is when pride can slip in, when we manage to convince ourselves that we are better or more deserving than another human being.

But get this—if guilt leads to pride, what does pride lead to? Wouldn't it be hypocrisy—propping ourselves up to be someone we're not? We can become quite skilled at hiding beneath a veneer of respectability, keeping our sins hidden from view.

Continuing with this progression, if guilt leads to pride, and pride to hypocrisy, what is the result of being a hypocrite? A constant burden, a heaviness, a weight on our souls of knowing who we really are inside. That gets wearisome. Worse yet, we begin not liking who we see in the mirror because we know the truth about ourselves.

Here is the real kicker. The weight of hypocrisy leads to rejection. Why wouldn't we want to reject an unattractive religious system laced with guilt, pride, pretense, and the burden of never being good enough? This is what many of us felt when we left home for college or started a career path. We said good-bye to a religious system that seemed more restricting than liberating, more judging than affirming.

Fortunately, there is a better way. In a word, it's *grace*—God's grace—the undeserved good and unearned favor that comes from God, having nothing to do with our performance. Grace is God accomplishing for us and in us what we cannot construct on our own.

Grace wipes out guilt as Christ forgives our sins and removes our shame. Grace eliminates pride when we realize it's not about how good we are but about how good God is. Grace does away with hypocrisy because God loves us for who we are, not for someone we're pretending to be. And grace replaces the burden of rule-keeping with the liberating power of love. God's relentless love for us is grace in its most powerful form. Listen to this invitation from Jesus:

"Come to me, all you who are weary and burdened, and I will give you rest. Take my yoke upon you and learn from me, for I am gentle and humble in heart, and you will find rest for your souls. For my yoke is easy and my burden is light." (Matthew 11:28-30)

What soothing words for those of us staggering under an unmanageable load derived from self-imposed expectations. Jesus is giving us his invitation to lay our burdens down and find emancipating rest for our souls. His gentle appeal comes to those of us who are tired of carrying the heaviness of life on our own. Jesus invites us to lay our heads on his shoulder, drawing strength and affirmation from him. He is offering us his gifts of grace—his mercy, his forgiveness, his salvation, his life becoming ours.

I pray that you would allow more of God's grace to abound in your life's journey. Life is better when Jesus is shouldering the load with you. The Lord will teach you how to have a less encumbered spirit by reminding you that you need not carry the weight of the world on your back. As God's grace expands in your life, you be set free to be more of the person you want to be and were created to be.

Grabbing Hold of Grace...

- Name a celebrity or other impressive person you've met or had a close encounter with. What was your impression of him or her?
- When it comes to your character, what is a strength? What is a weakness?
- What kind of church or religious background do you have, if any? What were the positives and negatives of that experience?
- Describe the concept of "grace" in your own words. What does grace mean to you personally?
- Identify an area in your life where you are most in need of grace right now. Take a moment to ask Jesus to lighten your burden.

12   deadliest catch

A Dose of Mercy

Working on a commercial shrimp boat in Alaska required a strong back and an even stronger stomach. The Bering Sea is no place for sissies, a fact well documented by the popular television series called *Deadliest Catch*. Instead of crab pots, the crew that I was part of dragged trawling nets attached to wire cables close to the ocean bottom. The nets billow open like gaping jaws and gobble up the masses of shrimp that thrive in these icy waters.

After two hours on the bottom, a powerful electric winch cranked the bulging nets toward the surface. Excitement mounted as the skipper estimated a haul of over 1000 pounds. When our catch emerged from the deep, it looked like a giant cork behind the boat. Seagulls circled for an easy snack as we winched the ball of wiggling creatures up and over the stern. Once hoisted in the air with a small crane, the net looked like an inverted hot air balloon ready to burst over our heads.

With the net swinging back and forth over the aft deck, the head crewman timed the release of the line that crimped the bottom closed. With a swift jerk of the line, an avalanche of shrimp spilled out and swamped the deck. We were suddenly wading in a knee-deep caldron of slithery pink crustaceans. Using snow shovels, we scooped all 1000 pounds of the ocean's bounty into the hold of the ship, iced down our catch, and then off-loaded our haul once back at the processing plant.

Laboring on a fishing boat wasn't easy, but working on the docks back at the harbor was no picnic either. The foreman greeted us greenhorns with a wry smile and told two of us to climb into a large steel bucket attached to an overhead crane. I knew we were doomed. While being lowered into the hold of a crab boat, I watched my life slipping away.

Stepping out of the bucket, my partner and I stood on a mountain of live, ornery Dungeness crabs. With nothing but rubber gloves for protection, we'd grab as many crabs as we could and drop them in the bucket. When the bucket was full, the crane operator hoisted up the load, emptied the crab for processing, and lowered the bucket for us to fill again, and again, and again.

We measured progress by how many inches or feet separated our heads from the deck above us. As the heap of crab got lower, we sunk deeper into the clammy, foul-smelling belly of the ship's steel hull. This mind-numbing labor would be interrupted by a scream when a crab locked on to a finger or thumb like a vise grip. Unchristian-like words resounded in the steel prison below while men in pain broke off the menacing claw. At the end of the day, bloodied gloves came off to examine the inventory of numerous flesh wounds and swollen fingers.

Compared to off-loading crab boats, processing halibut was a breeze. A conveyor belt delivered the fish from the boat to the processing area. Grabbing one of these bad boys by the gill enabled me to position the fish just right under a large hydraulic guillotine. With a push of a button, the sharp blade came slicing down and it was *off with yer head!* Slicing off heads is known as "slugging" halibut. Once headless, the fish is weighed on the scales and the data recorded. That summer I weighed in fish ranging from 50-pound youngsters to over 300-pound giants.

For the most part, you had to create your own entertainment in this small fishing village on the Aleutian chain of islands. This nearly road-less, treeless island of tundra had no television, no newspaper, and no *Starbucks*. A ramshackle movie house made of corrugated steel and a tin roof did exist in the middle of the village. Wooden planks on cinder blocks served as the best seats in the house. Every other Friday a small plane would arrive with the mail and a movie. No one cared that they weren't delivering new releases because everything was a new release in that part of the world.

One Friday, *Fiddler on the Roof* was flown in and nearly everyone in town planned to attend the only showing at eight o'clock. I had been slugging halibut that day and didn't finish until 7:45 pm, but I really wanted to see the movie. With no time to go home and take a shower, what was a man to do? I wiped the halibut slime off my jacket the best I could and ran over to the movie house.

When you work in a smelly place long enough you become accustomed to the stench and no longer smell what, in fact, smells. Consequently, when I walked into the movie house I wasn't sure why people were turning their noses up in the air. Then it dawned on me—I really stank. I sat down in a corner of the movie shack as the people nearby moved as far from me as possible. A little embarrassed, I decided to stay and hoped they'd get used to the smell of fish slime. They didn't.

The next day, and for several days following, it was payback time. People walked by me in the village while holding their noses. I was awarded a can of deodorant in the cannery lunch room. The foreman assigned me to fish gut detail. Hoping for mercy, I got what I deserved instead—payback.

• • • • •

There are two principles having to do with mercy and justice that I find most people are in agreement about. First is that we want justice to be served—we want people to get what they deserve. We want persons who do wrong to be appropriately punished, and we want persons who do right to be appropriately rewarded.

Second, when it comes to me or you, we want more mercy than justice. We want others to get what they deserve but when it comes to ourselves, we want more leniency than severity. Whether it's with a police officer who pulls you over for running a red light, or whether it's with an IRS agents' interpretation of the taxes you owe, or whether it's smelling like a halibut in the movie house, you are hoping for sympathy and kindness—not harshness and punishment. We prefer mercy over justice any day.

We could add a third principle about life that is widely agreed upon—life is not fair. Certainly we want fairness. But as we like to remind our children, much of the time none of us gets what we think we deserve. As a matter of fact, we often get what we don't deserve. We don't like this, *except* in the case of not getting the penalty we know we should. This goes back to the truism that we love justice when it applies to others, but not so much when it applies to us. We prefer mercy over justice any day.

Do you know that God does too? Certainly God is a God of justice, and he will see to it in the end that everyone is judged fairly. But God prefers mercy, loves mercy, and honors mercy. Jesus said we reflect God's likeness when we are kind and understanding toward people. *"Be merciful, just as your Father is merciful,"* Jesus said. (Luke 6:36).

What's more, God's blessing is extended to those who take into account each other's defects in a spirit of forgiveness and grace. *"Blessed are the merciful, for they will be shown mercy,"* Jesus declared. (Matthew 5:7) God will bless us with his mercy when we extend to others the mercy we have received.

As if to reinforce how important this principle is, Jesus comes at it from another angle: *"Do not judge, or you too will be judged. For in the same way you judge others, you will be judged, and with the measure you use, it will be measured to you."* (Matthew 7:1, 2) To judge in this context means to condemn, criticize or blame. We are warned not to be critical of others, because when our time comes to be held accountable by God, we want God to be lenient with us. But we will be judged on the basis of how we have treated others—either by a standard of harshness or of leniency—especially towards those who have wronged us.

On a practical level, mercy and grace has to be operational in order for any relationship to endure. In the absence of mercy, our relationships will eventually go down in the flames of unending judgments and accusations. There is *always* some fault that we can identify in another human being once we get to know him or her. But for integrity's sake, we have to admit that we are also flawed and in need of as much mercy as any other human being. We may not be able to smell the stink as much as others around us, but it is definitely there.

There is a little poem attributed to Edward Wallis Hoch, Robert Louis Stevenson and others that aptly states:

There is so much good in the worst of us
And so much bad in the best of us
That it hardly becomes any of us
To talk about the rest of us

Previously, I described grace as God extending gifts to us that we don't deserve, such as his forgiveness and salvation. Mercy, on the other hand, is about God withholding what we do deserve, like judgment and condemnation. If we think we don't deserve this, we are fooling ourselves. The Bible clearly says *"...all have sinned and fall short of the glory of God."* (Romans 3:23) So, when we find ourselves in God's courtroom one day and the Great Judge is making decisions with perfect justice, complete fairness and without favoritism—what do we do? Your life and eternity, my life and eternity are on the line. What is going to happen?

If we did random interviews of people on the street as to how they think this will work out in the end, I think most would say something like this: "I hope I've done enough good to outweigh the bad so that God will accept me into heaven." A big problem with that idea is the inability to objectively rank or grade oneself. Like me in the movie house oblivious to my foul condition, we are often not the best judges of our own situation. Not only that, how good are we going to appear before a perfectly righteous and holy God? We will all look tainted by comparison.

Instead of standing before God someday with our list of good deeds in hopes of convincing him of our worthiness, what if we go back to what God offers—having nothing to do with trying harder or hoping we're good enough. What God offers is simply his mercy and purely his grace. If you are wondering why God would make such an undeserving offer, the answer is found throughout the Bible: *"The Lord is compassionate and gracious, slow to anger, abounding in love. He will not always accuse, nor will he harbor his anger forever; he does not treat us as our sins deserve or repay us according to our iniquities."* (Psalm 103:8-10)

The reason God is gracious and merciful is because this is consistent with his nature. If God was a heartless tyrant, we would not stand a chance. Thankfully, God is a loving Father who cannot help but have compassion on his children. Our challenge in this life is to be merciful as he is merciful. When we do that, we reflect more of who God is and what God does.

Life is so liberating when we are living under the influence of God's mercy and grace. We are freed from the emotional angst of trying to even the score or getting what we think we have coming to us. Most everything that is good in our world is wrapped up in a *"mercy and grace"* kind of package.

So many times I have found myself pleading for God's mercy, and praying for his strength—particularly when being tempted by something I know is not good for me. I had a shocking experience in Hawaii that tested my resolve in a way that I never saw coming. In the next chapter, I'll reveal how one decision could have altered my life forever—and not in a good way…

A Dose of Mercy…

- Can you think of a time people saw something about you that wasn't right, but you weren't aware of it and were embarrassed after the fact?
- Describe a situation when you knew you were in the wrong and you received the justice you deserved.

- Define "mercy" in your own words. Think of an occasion when someone was merciful with you. What did receiving mercy "feel" like?
- If there is someone you are being overly harsh or critical toward, in what way could you begin to extend more mercy to him or her?

13 hawaiian hookers
Temptation Happens

a nticipation of our first visit to Hawaii flooded our minds with images of golden sand, palm trees, waterfalls, warm ocean water, and snorkeling with tropical fish. The thought of hookers, prostitutes, women of the street, didn't even register. But on the island of Oahu, we discovered many attractions not highlighted in the tourist brochures.

Driving through the congested streets of Honolulu didn't come close to the idyllic Hawaiian scene I had in mind. Nor did I find "paradise" in the bustling Waikiki strip where our hotel was located. Later, my wife Debbie and I drove to the windward side of the island and found a slice of heaven on earth that met every expectation.

But while relaxing in our room on the second night of our stay, I looked at my watch. It was only nine o'clock. Here we sat watching TV on a beautiful Hawaiian evening. *We could be doing this at home.* "I want to go out for a walk," I announced to Debbie. "Do you care to join me?"

"No, I'd rather stay here and chill."

"Ok—I won't be out long." I hopped on the elevator, got out on the main level and stepped onto a busy sidewalk. Most of the shops were still open and the night-life was in full swing. I'm sure I fit the profile of the typical tourist strolling and gawking down the Waikiki strip.

As I stopped to look though a store-front window, a woman's voice whispered something into my ear. Yes, she was that close. And what she said sent a chill up my spine. In a smooth silky voice she asked, "Do you feel lucky tonight?"

I froze. What was happening? I slowly turned around and saw a beautiful young woman winking at me and smiling seductively. She appeared ready for a party in her stilettos, short skirt, revealing blouse, and little white shoulder-strap purse.

I'm not too street wise but on the other hand, I wasn't born yesterday. It suddenly dawned on me that for the first time in my pastoral career, I was being propositioned! I felt my face flush. I didn't know what to say or if I should say anything at all.

Crazy thoughts raced through my mind: *Should I ask her how I can get lucky? Should I ask her what she does for a living? Should I tell her what I do for a living?*

I quickly abandoned those thoughts and made one of the best decisions of my life. I said, "No, I don't feel lucky. I'm feeling quite uncomfortable." Then I quickly walked away.

I went back to our room, told my wife what had just happened, and we enjoyed a good laugh over the incident. But little did I know this would not be the end of the story.

A few years later, I made another trip to Honolulu to serve as the moderator for a pastor's conference. Debbie didn't accompany me for the business part of the trip, but flew over to join me on the last day in Oahu. From there we would hop over to Maui for a romantic Hawaiian getaway.

Arriving at the airport, Debbie got on a shuttle bus that took her to the hotel not far from where we had stayed on our first visit. I was on a lunch break enjoying that familiar stroll down the Waikiki strip, hoping to meet Debbie before my afternoon meetings.

I crossed the street just a block away from the hotel, and stepped onto the crowded sidewalk. I then heard that familiar question being whispered into my ear: "Do you feel lucky?"

I froze. Was this really happening again? But the voice in my ear sounded all too familiar. Sure enough, I turned around and there was a beautiful woman winking and smiling at me. It was Debbie! My wife! Just playing a little practical joke on her husband!

And this time, instead of wondering what to do, I took her in my arms without hesitation, and said to her with all my heart, "Yes, right now I'm feeling very lucky. What man wouldn't consider himself lucky to be married to a woman like you?"

• • • • •

As the two of us walked hand-in-hand though the streets of Honolulu, I thought about how blessed I was to have a marriage like the one we have. At the same time, I thought about how easily our relationship could be damaged. Many times I've replayed in my mind the encounter I had with that prostitute, and what could have happened had I said *yes* to her in a moment of weakness. I recognize how vulnerable I am, and how easily my natural desires could convince me to enjoy momentary pleasure, resulting in a lifetime of regret.

Even though I could pat myself on the back for not yielding to temptation in that situation, I am well aware of how a friendly relationship with another woman could lead to an inappropriate one. I fully realize and have often said, "Except for the grace of God I could be the one who sins." This is why I never point a finger at those who fall to temptation, but do grieve over wounds of those affected by relational indiscretion. I shudder to think of the hurt that sexual sin would cause my wife—the one to whom I've sworn my undivided loyalty and trust. I need God's strength and the protection of the Holy Spirit to keep my love for her unwavering and strong.

Perhaps like me, you have prayed the Lord's Prayer countless times—so many times that it has become a mundane ritual. But we can make this prayer fresh every time we pray it by thinking about the meaning of each phrase, and by personalizing the lines as much as possible. The following is an example of how to make the prayer more personal:

> My Father, who is in heaven,
> Your name is holy,
> May your kingdom reign in my life,
> And on this earth as it does in heaven.
> Thank you for my daily bread,
> And forgive me my sins.
> I now forgive those who have sinned against me.
> *And lead me not into temptation,*
> *But deliver me from evil.*
> For the kingdom is yours,
> And the power, and the glory forever. Amen.

Temptation can hit us at any time in a variety of forms. The ancients acknowledged this by developing a summation of seducing desires known as "The Seven Deadly Sins." In modern terminology, they are usually identified as: anger, greed, lust, pride, envy, laziness and gluttony. I look at this list and realize I'm not only capable of succumbing to every one of these evils, but must confess that I'm guilty on all counts. This is why I am ever thankful for God's grace, mercy and love.

Still, these sins were called "deadly" for a reason. We know that any one of these evils can inflict great harm on ourselves and in our relationships. Whether you are a new Christian or have been a Christ-follower for many years, none of us is immune from these forces of seduction. Be aware that the evil one loves to attack an area of weakness just at the point when you have made a decision to take God more seriously or to follow Christ more devoutly. The good news is that with Jesus in your life, you can resist the devil. As the Bible says, *the one who is in you is greater than the one who is in the world.*" (I John 4:4b)

Here's more good news—there is no sin in being tempted. Even Jesus was tempted—and beat it! In the strong name of Jesus, we can beat temptation too. Please don't think anything is wrong with you when you are being tempted. This is a normal part of the Christian life. What is truly sweet is when we hold onto our convictions, resist temptation and know we just won a victory. There is great reward when we do this: calm replaces anger, contentment replaces greed, love replaces lust, humility replaces pride, gratitude replaces envy, energy replaces laziness, and moderation replaces gluttony. Each time we win a battle, we are closer to winning the war. Life is better.

Recently, Deb and I visited the Big Island and paddled kayaks across Kealakekua Bay to visit the Captain Cook Monument. We were told dolphin sightings were common in the bay and sure enough, we started seeing them—lots of them. Several groups of spinner dolphins were porpoising, leaping, and spinning as tourists sat in their kayaks and watched the show.

I came prepared with my snorkel, mask and fins and slid off the kayak to watch the underwater performance. But the coolest thing of all happened when Deb was sitting in the kayak and I was resting at the surface. With my mask in the water, I saw a dolphin break away from the pod, and swim upwards directly under us. I lifted my head out of the water, and said to Debbie, "Watch this!"

Immediately the dolphin rocketed out of the water a paddles' length away from us, cleared the water by ten feet, spun in circles four or five times, arched his back and did a perfect nose-dive back into the water! Then, as if he was applying for a job at Sea World, he began showing off. After that initial leap and spin, he did it again, and again, and again, and again! In fact, he didn't know when to quit. Debbie counted ten leaps, then fifteen, then twenty, then thirty, and finally stopped counting at about thirty-five leaps. That silly mammal had to be dizzy.

Paddling back to where the turquoise blue water met lush green foliage on shore, we both felt "lucky." More than that, we felt blessed, thanking God for each other and for every good gift our Father sends our way. The Lord has a way of enfolding us in his mercy and upholding us by his strength. Best of all, he gives us treasured relationships where he teaches us how to love, judgment free. And when that love is tested, relationships can become even stronger and more committed than ever.

Temptation Happens...

- In what ways do marketers and the media use temptation to serve their purposes?

- Of the "Seven Deadly Sins" which one(s) are you most susceptible to?
- Identify a specific instance, if you can, when you were tempted and beat that temptation. What helped you do that?
- Holding onto the truth that Christ has power and authority over evil, practice praying this daily prayer: "And lead me not into temptation, but deliver me from the evil one. Amen."

14 the nanny

There's Nothing Like Love

"What's wrong, honey?" I asked.

"Nothing's wrong, Dad," said my fourteen-year-old daughter Julia.

"Well, why are you looking so sad?"

"I'm not sad, Dad. I'm fine."

"Did something happen at school today?"

"Dad!" Julia fired back. "Are you hard of hearing? I told you I'm fine, so quit bugging me!" End of conversation.

My wife and I agree that raising a daughter tested our sanity far beyond what it took to raise two boys. Aaron and Nathan provided their own set of parental challenges, but their issues seemed less complicated than Julia's. Not only that, but it seems when most girls turn thirteen they not only think they're more intelligent than their parents but pretty much omniscient too.

Thankfully, Julia never got into serious trouble, made decent grades in school, and chose good friends also. But there was a time during her high school experience that I look back on as "the scary years." For whatever reason, Julia was shutting down and not letting me into her world at all. Sometimes she would open up to her mother, but often their conversations lead to arguments. We so wanted to be supportive parents during this vulnerable time in her life when making a bad choice was so easy to do. I worried a lot, and had to acknowledge that I had far more questions than answers.

To be honest, I saw a lot of myself in my daughter. During my growing up years, I was independent, self-assured, rebellious, and always choosing my own path—just like Julia. Now that she is thirty, I can see how these traits are serving her well in a competitive business world where only the strong survive. But as a young girl, these characteristics were not tempered by maturity, and as parents, we were either throwing up our hands in resignation or on our knees in prayer.

All of this came to a head one day when my frustration over our inability to communicate was at an all-time high. I was at a point where I was ready to do anything—I mean *anything* to get my daughter to open up to me. This resulted in an episode of Merritt parental lore that will forever go down as either an act of absolute genius, or more likely, an act of utter desperation.

On that inglorious day, I faced my daughter. "Julia, what will it take for you to talk to me? I feel you are shutting me out of your world. I worry about you, and I just want you to let me know what is going on in your life, because I love you and care about you."

"There is nothing you can do, Dad. There is nothing to talk about." That was the response I expected, and I was in a quandary.

I racked my brain thinking of what I could do or say that would make any difference in our relationship. Then an idea came to me. In all the parenting books I'd ever read, never had I seen anything about the use of bribery. But I also believed that desperate times required desperate measures.

I knew Julia wanted a puppy. She had been begging about this for months, but her mom and I were opposed for the reasons any parent might be—the parents end up caring for the dog after the excitement of puppy ownership wears off in about two weeks. But I couldn't think of any other solution to this problem—and I panicked.

And so, I looked Julia in the eyes, and said those words that will forever go down in infamy: "Honey, will you talk to me if I buy you a puppy?"

As soon as those words left my lips it was as if the fairy godmother had waved her magic wand. Julia's face lit up in a way that I hadn't seen in months. Her mood instantly shifted from dejection to delight. "Really Dad? Would you buy me a puppy?"

"Yes—but only under one condition. I will buy you a puppy if you promise to communicate regularly, and just talk about things. Ok?"

"Ok!" she said.

"Promise?"

"Yes, I promise."

Maybe I was a genius after all. But I soon found out my wife didn't think so. When I told her about the deal I struck with our daughter she said, "You did what? Without my input? A puppy? Why not a new dress or something? What were you thinking?" Looking back, I can see why she was upset. But at the time I wondered why women were so complicated.

Julia and I drove to a house after school one day where she had a choice of seven cream-colored puppies. She chose the runt of the litter, a Cocker Spaniel she named *Shasta*. She loved her puppy, and it did make an incremental difference in our communication— at least for a while. But for the record, I am not recommending bribery as a parenting principle.

Two years later, Julia's sixteenth birthday was rapidly approaching. I decided this was an opportunity to do something special I hoped would shore up our hit-and-miss communication patterns. I didn't know how she would respond to a daddy-daughter getaway, but I thought it was worth a shot.

We sat down at a local coffee shop. "How exciting that you are turning sixteen soon," I said. "I have an idea for you to think about. What if we took a trip somewhere for your birthday— just the two of us? We could pick a weekend, and fly anywhere you want to go—anywhere in the continental United States. What do you think?"

"Really? Sure. That would be fun, Dad."

Her reply made me so happy that I wanted to "high-five" her. But I didn't want to overreact so I hid my enthusiasm. "Do you have any thoughts about where you want to go?"

"I want to go to Hollywood," she said without hesitation. "I want to watch a TV show or movie being produced. Can we do that?"

Like many young girls, Julia's dream was to become a movie star some day. Fortunately, I had a friend who worked as a set designer in Culver City, California where many of the syndicated television shows are produced. He was working on *The Nanny*, starring Fran Drescher. He said he'd be happy to host us for a visit.

Julia and I landed at the Burbank Airport, hopped in a rental car and drove to the MGM Studios. We found the warehouse building where *The Nanny* was being filmed, and a guard promptly escorted us back stage. We met my friend who walked us over to where the giant cameras on wheels were ready for action. We began rubbing elbows with the camera crew, the directors and some of the cast. I watched my daughter's eyes light up as the set came to life with actors in place and the producer calling cues. This was magical!

But the best special effect for me was being there with Julia. We were connected, engaged, sharing this experience without any awkwardness. I so enjoyed these moments, being a proud dad of a lovely daughter who seemed okay just hanging out with me for a change.

There was a dinner break for the cast and crew that evening, and we were invited to join them in a large cafeteria. My friend introduced us to many of his colleagues including the producer of the show. He engaged Julia in conversation and discovered she was celebrating her sixteenth birthday.

"How long are you going to be here?" the producer asked.

"Well, we were planning to stay until the shoot is over for the day," I replied.

He then turned to Julia and asked, "How would you like to be an extra in the next scene?"

Julia did not hesitate. "Really? I would love that!"

"Consider it done!" In a matter of minutes Julia was being escorted backstage to a dressing room where a costume designer fitted her into a white formal gown. At the same time a makeup artist did some quick touch-ups to her face and hair. She was ready for her Hollywood debut—if only she could get her feet to touch the floor!

The scene was the wedding ceremony for the Nanny's daughter Maggie. Julia was acting as one of the invited guests and was strategically placed in an aisle seat. Her next lucky break happened during the actual filming. When the ceremony was finished and the wedding party came walking down the aisle, the Nanny spontaneously touched Julia on the shoulder. In a moment frozen in time, Julia turned her smiling face toward the camera and looked up at the Nanny who smiled back at her. More magic!

After filming was completed for the day, we got to meet Fran Drescher personally, and the snapshots we took proved this wasn't just a Hollywood fantasy. A few weeks later, our family gathered around the television in our living room to watch the wedding episode, wondering if Julia's appearance had survived the editing process. Sure enough, toward the end of the scene, there was our little movie star showing off her million dollar smile. Her dream had come true.

But there was an even larger dream that came true, at least for me. The connection that took place between me and my cherished daughter that weekend was priceless. It renewed my hope as a parent. More than once on that trip we reaffirmed our affections for each other. I whispered the words "I love you honey" into Julia's ears while watching takes and retakes of the show.

"I love you too, Dad," she replied. That's *all* I needed to hear. That's all I needed to know. That was the most important thing in the world to me—knowing she loved me, and that I loved her. As parents, this is what we hope for, long for and pray for. Because after all, love *"always protects, always trusts, always hopes, always perseveres."* (I Corinthians 13:7 NASB) Where there is love, all things are possible.

If you are a parent in what seems like a hopeless situation with your child, remember that your child has another Father and nothing is hopeless with him. God the Father cares about our children with a passion that goes far beyond our human ability to fathom. Our first job as parents is to love the Lord our God with our whole heart and mind. As we devote ourselves to the God who is fully committed to us, this does more for our children than any parental strategy we devise.

Asking God to bless our children, nurture our children, and embrace our children in his strong arms, relieves us of the burden of thinking the well-being of our children rests solely on us. It doesn't. There is a special place in God's heart for our children, and he will never give up on them. Our challenge is to trust the Lord by entrusting our children to him. As parents, we are not in this alone. God is very familiar with the challenge of parenting—we've given him plenty of experience!

There's Nothing Like Love...

- If you are a parent, describe your greatest success and your greatest failure in parenting.
- As our children grow up, the way we love them evolves according to stages of life. What specific ways have you expressed love to your kids in their different phases of growth.
- Try to draw as many similarities as you can between the parent/child relationship and the relationship God the Father has with us—particularly when it comes to love.
- Take a moment to entrust your children to the God the Father in prayer. Meditate on the truth that where God's love is, nothing is impossible.

15 saddle up
Love's Highs and Lows

y wife-to-be had no idea what she had just agreed to. Her hands were full planning the wedding— deciding about colors, dresses, flowers, music, order of the ceremony, cake, reception, and most difficult of all—who we would and wouldn't invite. Debbie had enough pressure. She didn't have time to worry about what happened afterward. So we both agreed that I would plan the honeymoon—a decision she still regrets some thirty-nine years later.

My main responsibility at the wedding was showing up—and I'm glad I did. I married the most wonderful woman imaginable that warm summer day in Minnesota. But like most guys, the wedding didn't excite me as much as what I hoped would happen *after* we tied the knot. I had big plans.

We cut the cake, tossed the garter, dodged the rice, jumped in the car and took off. We had 1000 miles to cover before arriving at our mountain cabin in Estes Park, Colorado. And so, we put about 200 miles behind us on the first night of our honeymoon. What was I thinking? *Road trip!* That's what I was thinking.

We found the cozy chalet in our mountain paradise to be perfect, and I set my agenda into motion with enthusiasm. Four days of adventure lay ahead of us. We both love to play golf so this activity for day one pleased Debbie. But from her perspective, the honeymoon started going downhill from there.

I eagerly anticipated the trout fishing excursion planned for day two, though it required a semi-difficult hike up to a beautiful mountain lake. I enjoyed every cast and every fish that came out of the crystal-clear waters but discovered my wife wasn't feeling the romance in this. I knew I needed to make it up to her on day three by creating a romantic memory that would last a lifetime. Little did I know that day three would put to the test the "for better or for worse" clause in our marriage vows.

Even though my wife is afraid of horses, I thought a gentle horseback ride up a mountain trail would help her conquer her fear. Again, what was I thinking? She got on that horse out of sheer love and devotion to me, but that would be the last time she'd do that— "for as long as we both shall live."

As we saddled up, the trail master offered to accompany us as our guide. But having a crusty old ranch hand along as chaperone was not my idea of a good time. I told him that I had vast horseback riding experience. I lied.

The horses seemed amiable enough as they trotted along the familiar trails leading up to Twin Sisters, a mountain peak at the 11,000-foot level. I tried to reassure my wife by looking back at her with adoring grins. "Isn't this fun, honey?" She responded with a weak smile.

Before long the trail turned to switchbacks as the mountainside steepened. The horses labored more heavily but plodded along at a steady pace—until we encountered an unexpected obstacle. It was early June, so we were the first ones to use the trail that spring and the first to discover several blown-down trees blocking the trail.

"John, let's turn around and go back," pleaded Debbie.

Because I'm not a "turn around and go back" kind of guy I tried to assure my bride. "Honey, we just need to get off our horses and I'll lead them around the fallen trees."

Reluctantly, she climbed off her horse. I then tied mine to a tree and began leading hers around the obstacles. But while guiding her horse, mine reared his head and managed to pull his reins free. In a flash, he turned around trotted down the mountainside at a quick pace. This horse was headed back to the barn!

"John, your horse is loose!" Debbie screamed.

Quickly, I tied her horse to a tree and then raced straight down the steep slope, jumping over fallen trees and boulders. I gained ground on the horse by cutting across the switchbacks. Half running and half sliding, I came crashing out of the brush at a place in the trail just below the oncoming animal.

There I stood in the middle of the trail with the horse barreling towards me, hoping and praying he would stop. I waved my arms over my head. "Whoa! Whoa!" Thankfully, he came to a halt just an arms-length away. I took the reins. "Nice horsy." Then I hoisted myself onto the saddle.

I rode back up to my young bride standing alone in the middle of the Rocky Mountains with an animal she didn't like or trust. She was not happy. "*Now* can we turn around and go back?"

"Perhaps that would be a good idea. But we are so close to the summit and that gorgeous view of Longs Peak across the valley. Let's go to the top and then head back down."

She didn't answer but halfheartedly followed me up to the snow-covered peak. The view was spectacular but the romantic moment I had in mind flopped. No high-fives, no hugging and kissing each other at the top, no giddy conversation as our boots crunched through the snow back to where our horses were tied. Just uncomfortable silence.

We exchanged few words as we plodded down the mountainside together, listening to the steady *clop, clop, clop* of the horses retracing their steps. Once back at the barn, the trail master asked if we had had any problems. "No, no problems," I replied. Debbie rolled her eyes.

• • • • •

Love is a precarious venture for flawed human beings to embark upon. So much can go wrong even when you think you are doing your best to make a relationship work. The explanations as to why love fails have filled volumes, but it boils down to a common reality—self-interest gets in the way. Because I want to do what I want and gratify my own desires as I please, putting someone else's interests above my own becomes extremely challenging. When you come to this realization, it can cause you to wonder if love is worth the risk, the hard work, the inconvenience, the inevitable hurt and disappointment.

And yet, what is life without love? No life at all. Whether it is love in a marriage or in a friendship or in a family relationship—to love and to be loved is the greatest source of enjoyment in the world. Love requires us to go beyond ourselves and enter into the life and soul of another—just as God does with us. As we learn how to love more like God loves us, life is richer, happier, more pleasurable. And we become healthier people when we learn to love.

Once Debbie and I were able to talk about it, we learned some things about ourselves that would serve our marriage well for years to come. I learned how to sincerely apologize. She learned how to forgive, although she's still working on how to *forget*. But I understand her much better now, and we are able to look back and laugh as she tells the story over and over again at my expense.

There is one thing about love you can count on—it tests you. Love has a way of getting under your skin and finding out what you are made of. This is not always comfortable but if you allow love to do its work, you become a better person—a person who more clearly reflects the nature of God.

When I officiate at wedding ceremonies, I often speak of how love will test a marriage by pointing out the four expressions of love used in the New Testament. We are challenged in the English language because our word "love" is too broad and isn't adequate in defining the numerous dimensions of love. But in the original Greek language of the New Testament, there were at least four words used to describe the multiple facets of love.

A word used by the Greeks is *"eros"* from which we get the word "erotic." We imagine this is the kind of love when Adam first laid his eyes on Eve—a wild, steamy, romantic, glassy-eyed sort of love. This powerful emotion is what stirs sexual attraction and is what is meant when someone says they have "fallen in love." But as important as this aspect of love is, it comes and goes, ebbs and flows. Love that fails to rise above the emotional level will remain immature and will not last.

Next is the word *"philia,"* a term the Greeks used to depict "brotherly love." This is the love of friends, of sharing life together as companions, where you are close enough that you can call each other *"brother"* or *"sister."* This love is tested when you are called upon to be a friend when it's inconvenient or when you don't feel like it. As you set self-interest aside and practice loving your friend as yourself, your love demonstrates a deepening maturity.

A third expression of love is "storge," referring to compassion applied "in sickness and health". This is demonstrated in a nurturing, empathizing way that serves to bind up the wounds and disappointments of someone you care about. This test of love is met when you simply choose to be present, or be a good listener, or walk patiently through a trial with someone, being merciful and understanding.

The fourth dimension of love is "agape." The Greeks considered this the supreme form of love because it is one of choice, expressing a will to love. This is a *no matter what you do or what you say, I'm going to love you and you can't stop me* kind of love. Agape is a decision you make and choose to honor when "better" turns to "worse." This is the same love God expressed toward us when he sent his Son to pay the penalty for our sins and to die in our place. Yes, agape love is tested to the limit when one lays down his or her life for another.

We may think that bailing on a relationship when it becomes too difficult is the way to get back our life and freedom. But it's not. Liberating joy in life comes as we're able to persevere in a relationship because that person matters deeply to us, even to the point of giving up our life for the other.

"My command is this," Jesus said. *"Love each other as I have loved you. Greater love has no one than this: to lay down one's life for one's friends."* And why does Jesus give his followers this obligation to love, life for life? Not to take away our joy but to obtain it. *"I*

have told you this so that my joy may be in you and that your joy may be complete." (John 15:11-13)

While most of our attempts to love will fall short of Christ's perfect love for us, the decision to love, however inadequate, has the power to change minds and heal relationships. Love softens our hearts and saves us from toxic self-absorption. And as that happens, we are able to enjoy our cherished relationships more, and our love for God deepens. We find that we are capable of loving the unlovely, the undeserving, and the unappreciative. When we choose to love in this way, miracles can happen and the world is changed.

Love's Highs and Lows...

- Define "love" in your own words.
- In what way do you think our culture has cheapened the concept of love or made it into something shallow?
- Do you agree that self-interest is a big reason why loving others can be so difficult? What has helped you put the interests of others ahead of your own?
- Name a time when your attempt to love failed. Name a time when your attempt to love succeeded. What was the difference?
- Describe the joy that love in a relationship has brought to your life.
- Is there someone who is difficult to love in your life? What do you think Jesus might be asking you to do about that?

16 the mad egyptian
No Fear This Day

navigating the streets of downtown Cairo is not for the faint of heart. Our tour group watched in amazement as our bus driver maneuvered around traffic jams and jay-walking pedestrians. How could he avoid an accident in such chaos?

We were heading for the Church of Saint Sergius—our destination for the day—when the inevitable occurred. This site is said to be the traditional place where Joseph, Mary, and infant Jesus fled from King Herod who was intent on finding Jesus and killing him. But our progress came to a halt when we felt a subtle bump from the rear of the bus followed by someone yelling and pounding on the side of the vehicle.

As our driver opened the door to investigate, the cab driver, who had struck our bus from behind, reached in and grabbed our driver by the neck. The bus driver tried to resist the assault while the two shouted and cursed at each other.

Being a hulk of a man, the cab driver managed to drag our driver out of the bus and throw him to the ground. I had wondered earlier in the day why it was necessity for us to have an armed guard on board riding in the passenger seat. I no longer wondered about that as I watched the cab driver step onto the bus and lunge for the ignition keys while the guard tried to stop him. Sitting directly behind the driver's seat, my wife and I watched in horror as these burly men began to fight. While at each other's throats, our guard wrestled and shoved the cab driver out of the bus.

Once outside, the two continued to shout and threaten each other with fists. The mad Egyptian raged out of control. A group of locals who had surrounded the man tried to reason with him to no avail. Though he had struck our vehicle from behind, he violently resisted any suggestion that he was at fault.

Meanwhile, back on the bus, people were terror-stricken. Some in the group prayed while others looked at the shocking scene unfolding in the streets. Here we were, a little island of American foreigners surrounded by a nation of people in complete control over us. For folks used to the advantages of being in the majority and of being a United States citizen, this was an unsettling position. We sat like trapped birds in a cage—frightened, powerless and vulnerable to anyone wanting to take advantage of the situation.

The anxiety level among the group rose as we watched the altercation continue. Finally, with torn shirts and bloodied faces, our driver and guard were able to pull away from the crowd. What a relief to see the door close, hear the engine start, and feel the bus moving away from that scene. But our relief was short-lived as another bizarre situation put us on the edge of our seats once again.

Our driver raced through the streets faster and faster, zigzagging his way in and out of traffic. We were all still shook up over what had just happened. I was about to ask him to please slow down. But then someone on the left side of the bus yelled out, "Look, the cab driver is chasing us!"

Driving like a maniac, the cab driver caught up and kept pace with us. I wondered how this could be happening—a chase scene in Cairo? But these were not stunt men and this was not Hollywood. After a nail-biting ten minutes with numerous near-miss accidents, we pulled up to a police station. Our driver and the cab driver got out of their respective vehicles, and the shouting match started all over again.

Fortunately this confrontation didn't last long as the cab driver had no qualms about getting into the faces of the police officers who proceeded to haul him off to jail. We learned later that drugs contributed to his anger issues—yes, a cab driver on drugs! We were all thankful to have emerged from this ordeal without suffering bodily harm.

• • • • •

As leader of our tour group, this was not the introduction to the Holy Land that I had in mind. My people knew the risk of traveling in Egypt just months after violent protests in Tahrir Square toppled President Hosni Mubarak. The evidences of the people's uprising were still visible. We saw cars that had been burned to the ground and government high-rise buildings that had been torched and abandoned. Still, no one expected our tour bus full of Americans to be attacked.

If you are an American citizen, you'd probably agree that we are the most blessed people on earth. We enjoy so many advantages, freedoms, luxuries and opportunities that other people in the world only dream of. Every time I go to another country and come back to the U.S., I thank God for the privilege of living here.

But there is an important caution about being a Christian in America. The particular danger is when we only see an Americanized expression of Christianity. We easily become isolated from what God is doing in other countries and sometimes lack awareness of the vibrant Christian presence in diverse parts of the world. The challenge we face is being more globally aware of where other Christians live, what their special challenges are, how we can pray for them, and how to identify with them as fellow believers.

Many American Christians don't know, for example, there are Christians and churches throughout the Middle East in countries such as Egypt, Israel, Iraq, Iran and Syria. If we were more informed, we would know that many nations in Africa and Latin America are predominantly Christian. And in countries where Christians are in a distinct minority, it is humbling to see their authentic and bold faith being expressed while facing the realities of extreme poverty and religious persecution.

This is why I encourage Christians living in the United States to go to a third-world country, not as a tourist on vacation. Consider going on a mission trip for a week or two with the goal of becoming a more informed global Christian. Get involved, ask questions, get your hands dirty, and read about what God is doing in other parts of the world. Our experience in Egypt became a lesson in spiritual formation for many in the group. Some began thinking globally for the first time in their lives.

When we got off the bus at the Church of Saint Sergius, I saw the look of solemn apprehension on the faces of my fellow travelers. As we walked inside the church, I heard whispers that at least one in my group was ready to go home on this our second day of a two-week trip to the Middle East. As the leader, I knew I had to do something to address what had just happened.

I found a church overseer in this ancient place of worship, and asked if we could meet as a group in a quiet place somewhere in the building. The elderly gentleman kindly guided us to an area in the sanctuary where he gave us his blessing and we sat down. None of us will ever forget those special moments in the corner of that church where Christ-followers known as Coptic Christians have worshiped for centuries. "Coptic" was a native form of the Egyptian language going back to the third century that is still used in the liturgy of the Coptic Church of Egypt.

I asked God for the words to say to the group, and began by thanking God that we were all alive and physically unharmed. I then reminded them of the place where we were sitting—the place where our Lord sought refuge from persecution some 2000 years ago. I also mentioned that we were in a location where Christians have suffered persecution for generations due to their minority status. Here in this place we had the unusual opportunity to unite ourselves with the Holy Family, with the minority races and religions of the world, with all those who suffer injustice, and to pray for them.

As gently as possible I suggested to our group that we had a choice of how we were going to react to the traumatic incident that took place in the streets just minutes earlier. We could become self-focused and feel sorry for ourselves, or we could give our thoughts and emotions over to the plight of others around us who feel threatened every day. Instead of being typical American tourists reacting to a threat to our safety, perhaps for the first time we could truly identify with the poor and the oppressed who gathered here every Sunday, sitting in the very seats we were occupying—yes, our fellow Egyptian believers.

I could not have been more proud of our group as we prayed for each other, for the poor, for the oppressed and for the powerless. After sharing communion together, we ventured out again. We did so with noticeable timidity, staying close to one another for the support we needed. Gradually our collective fear melted into gratitude, because that brush with violence transformed some of our perspectives. Conversations with local people became more meaningful and our prayers for them had a deeper authenticity. We were seeing the world with a different set of eyes.

On our final day in Egypt two Cairo squad cars parked alongside our bus in front of the Ramses Hilton Hotel. Initially we wondered if more trouble was brewing. To the contrary, we were relieved to find out that the Egyptian authorities had decided to grant us some royal treatment. All day long a dedicated police escort never let us out of their sight. They followed our bus, stopping where we stopped, got out to create paths through traffic, and shadowed our little group like the FBI does for the president. The government was sending us a nonverbal message that said: *We're sorry for your trouble—please come back again soon.*

This was a reassuring and hopeful gesture. Hope is an elusive commodity in this part of the world where the "Arab Spring" is in full bloom. But may we not forget the courageous Christian community serving as a witness of Jesus Christ in this proud land of rich biblical tradition. God and his people are there, and because this is true there is always reason to hope—always.

No Fear This Day...

- Identify a time when you were being threatened by someone's rage. How did you respond or what did you do?
- If you have ever been to a third world country, describe the contrasts between life in that country to life in America.

- What challenges, if any, do you think goes along with being a Christian in America? What do you think it means to be a global Christian?
- What exposure have you had with Christians in another country? Is there anything intentional you are doing or could be doing to identify with the poor and oppressed in the world?

17 mutiny
Always a Reason to Hope

om, I'm scared," said our four-year-old, Juila.
"I'm scared too," said her mother.
That's not what I needed to hear just hours into our fourteen-day sailing adventure. To feel safer, Julia went into the cabin below, hid under some blankets, got seasick, and threw up all over our bedding. My vision of a happy family sailing off into the sunset plummeted.

The charted course for our twenty-five foot *O'Day* sailboat would take us round-trip from our home in Sturgeon Bay, Wisconsin to Mackinac Island, Michigan—about 350 nautical miles. I had a young crew—Aaron was nine, Nathan was six and Julia was four—and not all of them were eager to sign on for the voyage. But I took a family vote, ignored the abstentions and the plan steam-rolled ahead. I figured this is what a good father does—create family vacations and precious memories whether I had willing participants or not.

But after sailing out of the harbor on the first day, we rounded a point and entered Green Bay where thirty-mile-per-hour North winds and five-foot seas slammed us head on. With great difficulty we tacked into the wind. When a strong gust caused the boat to list on its side, my boys tried to be brave but huddled like chicks around their brooding mother. The trip had barely begun and I was losing the confidence of my crew members.

Instead of traveling the thirty miles planned for that day, we managed a disappointing twelve miles. I pulled into the first harbor offering protection, and listened all night to the irritating *clank, clank, clank* of the hardware on the lines blowing against the mast. I prayed for more favorable seas by morning.

Day two provided some promise as the wind subsided considerably. No one said they were scared as we sailed along— and no one threw up. That evening we tied up at a lovely little island at the end of the Door Peninsula where the boys caught fish off the dock. We grilled hamburgers on the aft deck and enjoyed "s'mores" around a camp fire on the beach. The angst of the previous day seemed to be fading from the memories of my young sailors.

But then day three dawned. I remember it as the day hope died. Bad weather rolled in again, and it appeared that our boat named *Heaven Bound* would soon be "home bound." I painted a bleak picture in the Captain's log of what happened:

August 6, 9:30pm. Today I've decided that my goal for this family adventure is far too ambitious. We pushed off of Rock Island and headed westward. Once away from the leeward side of Washington Island, southerly winds gusting to forty-

five mph slammed into us. Waves rolling up to ten feet pushed us astern. I reefed the main sail and ran with the jib sail sending us up one trough and down the other.

My crew panicked as we climbed up each mountain of water and slid down into the valley on the other side. After a wild eighteen-mile ride, I ducked into a well-protected cove on the NE corner of Summer Island, tossed the anchor overboard, and slumped over in exhaustion.

My family is sleeping as I write. I have not told them yet, but I have concluded that the hope of reaching Mackinaw Island is all but dashed. Making it to our destination would require a fifty-five mile crossing over the open water of northern Lake Michigan to Beaver Island. As I listen to the wind whistling and distant waves crashing, I know that if I choose to proceed I will have mutiny on my hands. Tomorrow we will try to turn back.

But when we awoke the next morning we heard something strange—silence! The storm had passed. A new day welcomed us with sunshine and a favorable breeze. My brave mates were ready to push forward, covering the most miles in a single day of our entire expedition. The first line I penned in the log the evening of August 7th said: *What a difference a day makes!* I wrote that phrase from the slip assigned to us by the Harbor Master at Beaver Island following a fifty-five mile passage. This was a turning point where our dreams were resurrected and our hope restored.

The next day we sailed under the impressive Mackinac Bridge and finally into the welcoming harbor of Mackinac Island. We tied up to the dock and sprinted downtown to do what people do on that island—eat fudge! Two words from the Captain's log dated August 8 tells the tale: *Mission Accomplished!* While we still had to sail back home, my seasoned crew was transformed from cowering landlubbers to gallant sailors. They now believed they were capable of sailing around the world!

• • • • •

Can you remember a day in your life when it seemed like hope had died? Hope may have been scuttled in your endeavor to obtain a college diploma, land a job, find love, close a business deal, or even take your relationship with God to the next level. Perhaps you allowed critics and naysayers to mutiny hope. They did their their best to diminish your dreams and weaken your faith. I understand. Like sailing with a young family across unchartered waters, your confidence may ebb and flow with the unpredictable winds that billow your sails.

There will be many times in your life when you cannot see hope on the horizon. But at the moment when all seems lost, a favorable breeze can spring up and propel you onward in pursuit of what you believe is possible. Keeping hope alive can be difficult, especially in these modern times when economic, political, and societal pessimism is rampant. But we must keep in mind that our hope as Christians doesn't depend on how the economy is doing or how our government is performing. With God charting our course, there is always cause for hope, always reason to persevere, and always the promise of a new day.

Just to be clear, hope is not merely wishing for good luck instead of bad luck. Rather, hope is the anticipation arising out of a confident belief that all things are possible as you press on with God leading the charge. When facing a daunting challenge remember that God is not worried, frustrated, fearful or uncertain. He simply asks that you trust him and take full advantage of his ability to show you the way forward.

If you find it hard to be hopeful these days, I have a suggestion. Create opportunities to spend time with children. If you are a parent with kids at home, you can do this every day. Granted, what you see in your children doesn't always encourage you. But there are those moments when your kids inspire you with their faith, their resilience and their strength. I see this in our grandchildren. My spirit soars when I am with them. I see in Abigail, Brady, Logan, Reese and Callie such promise. They are living examples of all that is right, good, and true in the world.

Whether or not you have children at home, I encourage you to find a time and place to interact with other young people— maybe in the youth department at your church. If you want to do something really courageous, start hanging out with middle or high school students. As you take the time to get to know them and learn what makes them tick, you will be inspired. No matter what their backgrounds or family situations, you will find in most all of them a built-in playfulness, curiosity, imagination and hopeful trust that is contagious.

Jesus welcomed little children into his arms saying, *"the kingdom of God belongs to such as these."* (Mark 10:14) How refreshing for Jesus to disengage for a moment from the cynical adult world by surrounding himself with little ones who radiated an infectious spirit of hope. Jesus commended their childlike humility and faith, which enabled them to embrace God's rule and reign over their lives. We would do well to follow their example.

I remember what happened after surviving that Lake Michigan storm while anchored up at Summer Island. My wife was not a happy camper, and I was discouraged because the adventurer in me felt defeated. But our two young boys had other things on their minds.

"Dad, can we go skinny dipping?"

mutiny | 111

"Sure." We had the cove to ourselves.

After a refreshing swim, they wanted to shoot their BB guns in the woods lining the shore. So we rowed our dingy to the beach and did just that. Watching them brought a smile to my face. They were living in the moment. They weren't concerned about tomorrow. *Pop* went the BB gun. They were off on their own care-free adventure.

Soon we would be on a voyage of another kind—moving the family from Wisconsin to California to launch a new church. Debbie and I were concerned about the impact the move would have on our children. We worried about how they would adjust in new schools. But they made their adjustments and thrived. Aaron is now a youth pastor and family therapist. Nathan is a practicing anesthesiologist. Julia is a sales manager in the corporate world of San Francisco. We are amazed at who they are and what they have become—and they restore our hope.

Sometimes we need a different perspective than the one we are fixated on. The Bible advises us to *"…run with perseverance the race marked out for us, fixing our eyes on Jesus, the pioneer and perfecter of faith."* (Hebrews 12:1b, 2) I love the thought of Jesus being the "pioneer" of our faith. That means he is a great adventurer who blazed the trail of faith before us. Our job is to stay on that trail and not lose sight of Jesus. Nothing beats the adventure he has in mind for us. As long as he is plotting our course, we can push forward with confidence.

There will be times when you will be tempted to mutiny when you find that God is taking you on a journey that is neither safe nor predictable. You find your faith is being tested and your hope tried. But with each entry in your sailor's log, you'll find you are growing stronger, tougher, more mature, ready to take on larger challenges, leaving child's play behind. Through it all, you are achieving your goal of becoming a more mature man or woman of faith—and this satisfies your soul.

Always a Reason to Hope...

- Think of a situation involving your job, your family or an organization where mutiny was in the air. What happened?
- Reflect for a moment about the troubles that our nation and world faces. In your estimation, which of these problems seem nearly hopeless—and why?
- Define "hope" in your own words. Describe something that brings hope to your life right now.
- The Bible is full of hopeful promises. Take a moment to list a few of God's promises that mean the most to you.
- Describe a recent interaction with children or youth. What do you see in the next generation that instills hope?

18

abalone

Overwhelmed by Grandeur

S o John, what do you do?" asked a pastor from Chicago.
"I go abalone diving."
"You what?"
"I dive in the ocean for abalone."
"So, what on earth is an abalone?"

Sitting around the table that day were a dozen other pastors of large churches from across the country. Our facilitator asked us to talk about the recreational activities we enjoyed doing when we had a day off. The smell of salt water filled my nostrils as images of the ocean swirled in my head.

I decided to draw these clergymen out of their familiar turf of sermons, sacraments and saints into the unfamiliar surf of snorkels, swells and shells. Abalone are actually large sea snails with oval-shaped shells about the size of an outspread hand. These delectable gastropods can only be harvested by *free divers*—free of air tanks and regulators.

Donning wet suits, weight belts, mask, snorkel and fins, a diver must swim out from shore to where the water is twenty to thirty feet deep, take a deep breath, kick to the bottom, try to locate an abalone in a rocky crevice, pry his muscular foot off the rock with a small pry-bar, grab the unattached catch before the surge washes him away, and then kick like crazy back to the surface for a much-needed gasp of air.

The water can be quite dark at the bottom due to the thick fog on top and the kelp below that blots out sunlight along California's North Coast. Water temperatures range from a cold 55 degrees to an icy 46 degrees requiring hefty seven millimeter wet suits. Combined with other variables such as large swells, wind waves, underwater surge, poor visibility, sinus pressure, leg cramps and sea sickness puts this sport in the "extreme" category.

"What was your worst day of abalone diving?" a pastor asked.

The day my buddy and I were diving blind ranked among the worst. Putting our masks in the water was like putting your face in a bucket of gray water you just used to mop the floor. When swimming downward, we didn't know how deep we were. The rocky bottom would appear out of nowhere about an arm's length away. We should not have been in the water.

Luckily, I found one abalone and then another on successive dives. But after plucking the second one out of a rocky crevice, I floated away from the bottom and abruptly lost all visual reference points. Discerning up from down was impossible. Staring blindly into the chalky whiteness, my lungs cried out for oxygen as the seconds ticked away.

I forced myself to remain calm as the number one rule of free diving streamed from my memory bank. If you find yourself in trouble, release your weight belt. This action allows the buoyancy of your neoprene wetsuit to act as a life vest and will eventually float you to the surface.

While keeping that option in mind, I made a lightning-fast decision. I'd swim for a few seconds to what I thought might be the surface. If that didn't work, I'd dump my weight belt and float in the right direction. The path I selected at random turned out to be an angled route toward the surface. Just before releasing my weight belt, my head popped above the white-wash. Never had I gulped air so desperately.

Wasting no time swimming to shore, I scrambled out of the churning surf and up the rocky cliff. Once several feet above the turbulence, I sat down to rest and recover. The breakers crashed into the rocks below, sending tall plumes of spray into the air. Still shaking from my experience, I gazed in awe at the vastness and power of the mighty Pacific Ocean.

Swept away in wonder, my gaze turned into a trance-like state. The ocean's infinite nature overwhelmed me. I shrank in comparison, envisioning myself as nothing more than a drop in the bucket, a grain of sand, an infinitesimal plankton engulfed in immensity. Minuscule, insignificant, powerless—that's how I felt. Entertaining thoughts of my stature, importance or intelligence seemed utterly laughable to me. I was a speck of a man, sitting on the edge of unfathomable magnitude.

• • • • •

If you're like me, you've thought a lot about God—who he is, where he is, what he does and how we can describe him. We've no doubt heard attempts by well-intentioned people trying to explain the nature of God by reducing him into manageable sound-bites in order to wrap our small brains around his infinity. I am guilty of doing this myself. Countless times I have plumbed the depths of the divine, trying to express his enormity and complexity. In honest moments I will admit that God is a riddle inside an enigma wrapped around a conundrum.

Be honest. How many times have you thought or have been bold enough to say: *If I were God I could do a much better job of running the Universe than he's doing.* Usually thoughts like this stem from the frustration of seeing all that is not right in our world. We see the suffering of the innocent, the decline of moral standards, and the increased use of violence to make a statement. As society continues to worsen instead of improve, we may wonder why a God who is omnipotent, omniscient and omnipresent doesn't do more, act more, and intervene more in the name of truth, justice, love, and peace.

It is no sin to wonder what God is up to by allowing evil to run its course. But would we fault God for giving people the freedom to make unimpeded moral choices through the exercise of our human wills? Certainly God could impose his will on us and force everyone to do what is right, good and true at all times. But in that situation God would be a tyrant and we would no longer be human. Instead, God has implanted his moral sense into our souls and gives us the freedom to live according to his design or deviate from that as we choose.

What we must not lose sight of is that God is involved in the everyday affairs on earth. God does intervene and continues to make himself known in this world. And—get this—he does it *through us*! God is showing up and taking action every time we choose love over hate, truth over deceit, right over wrong. God chooses to do his work of overcoming evil with good by accomplishing his purposes through our God-honoring actions. In other words, if we wish to get a glimpse of what God is doing in the world then take a good look at a Christ-follower in action. We see God's ideals, God's purposes, God's plans being carried out by those whose love for the Lord is expressed in loving their neighbors as themselves.

That said, I still maintain that second-guessing God is absurd, especially when sitting on the shore of an ocean that contains species of plankton we don't know exist or why that even matters. Turns out that plankton matters to a group of scientists who recently completed a two-and-a-half year, 70,000-mile voyage around the world's oceans. They discovered 1.5 million species of plankton—twice the number previously known to exist. *(Data from Tara Oceans Project)*

These scientists are proposing that the functions of microscopic plankton—such as converting carbon dioxide into oxygen—may hold the secret as to whether or not the earth continues to be habitable for human beings. Sadly, they also found minute shreds of plastic that outnumbered the plankton, especially in the Antarctic. That is when my sarcastic side can't help but say, *and I suppose we think God should do something about that too!*

Frankly, I've tried playing God and it never goes well. I'm learning to embrace the mystery of God, concluding that an inability to understand him is no reason for rejecting him. Our cognitive abilities are but a drop from the ocean of his intelligence. If God was no bigger than what our minds can comprehend, he would not be worthy of our reverence and awe.

I've found that crawling out of the water like a drowned rat after diving in marginal conditions is a good cure for thoughts of transcendence. When I'm spitting out salt water and feeling like a washed-up piece of kelp, repenting of overinflated views of my significance comes easily. And praying the great prayer found in the book of Romans makes all the sense in the world:

*"Oh, the depth of the riches of the wisdom and knowledge
of God! How unsearchable his judgments, and his paths are
beyond tracing out! Who has known the mind of the Lord? Or
who has been his counselor? Who has ever given to God, that
God should repay them? For from him and through him and
for him are all things. To him be the glory forever! Amen."*
(Romans 11:33-36)

A highly intellectual man articulated that prayer. His name
was Paul, author of over half the books of the New Testament.
Saint Paul was uniquely qualified to declare that the God who is
over and above us, transcendent and sovereign, is worthy of our
worship and praise. The prayer reminds us that God knows what
he is doing—always has, always will.

The shore of an ocean is one of those places where God's
magnificence can wash over our souls. The Grand Canyon is
another place where you can find yourself swallowed up in the
grandeur of God. And that's where the next story will take us...

Overwhelmed By Grandeur...

- What is the most "extreme" activity or adventure you ever
  did? What made it extreme?
- Name a time when you felt very small due to the imposing
  nature of your surroundings or circumstances.
- What do you find most confusing or mysterious about
  who God is or what God does?
- The concepts of God's sovereignty and human will are
  often hard to reconcile. How do you explain the paradox
  of God being in control while humans are free to make
  choices?

- Perhaps you have been guilty of trying to "play God" or of thinking you can do a better job than he is doing. Consider repenting of those thoughts now and allow God to be God in your life.

19 lava falls
Compelled to Worship

b lack balloons and gag gifts reminding me of my mortality was not what I had in mind for my 50th birthday celebration. But how could I avoid an unwanted surprise party? I'm sure my wife and office staff had good intentions when they planned it. However, I wasn't going to stick around for this gala so I decided to escape to one of the most untraceable and unreachable chasms on planet earth I could think of—the Grand Canyon.

Three trusted friends and I descended on the Bright Angel Trail with other adventurers to the bottom of the mile-deep gorge where our rafts and crew were waiting. Most in the group boarded large oar boats controlled by the oarsman. My buddies and I hopped aboard a small paddle raft where negotiating rapids depended on our ability to execute orders barked out by our guide in the stern. Commands such as *hard forward, back paddle, high side* were maneuvers we quickly learned to perform.

"Rarely is anyone ever thrown out of the raft," our guide said. "But in the event that this happens, try to swim back to the raft. If that is not possible, float through the rapids on your back with your feet facing down-river. Is that clear?" We all nodded.

We questioned what she meant by "rarely" after losing people on three previous occasions when our raft was pounded by some of the hardest jolts and largest drops in the world of whitewater. After negotiating one of these rapids named "Little Bastard," our raft drifted into a back eddy and got caught in a wicked whirlpool. The power of the swirling current sucked a corner of the raft under water and took our strongest paddler with it. Like being flushed down a giant drain, he disappeared before any of us could grab him.

I watched in angst as one of my best friends with a wife and three small children vanished. Even with his life preserver strapped on, the hydraulic force kept him down for one of the longest minutes I've ever lived through. Finally we saw his hand, then the top of his head, and then his upper body bob like a cork to the surface.

We hauled him back into the raft and gave him time to catch his breath. "I would have surfaced sooner but my first attempt failed when my head hit the underside of the raft. I was sucked back down again," he said, "and spent a little more time in the turbulence of the 'green room.' That was spooky."

After this sobering experience, our post-rapid celebrations lost a bit of their swagger as we realized this river had the power to do anything it wanted with us—especially if we got too cocky. One rapid in particular created a sort of reverence among us—the granddaddy of them all, Lava Falls.

The guides didn't need to say a word. Their shift in demeanor informed us that we were about to encounter a force to be reckoned with. We parked our rafts on the shore and hiked to a vantage point to scout the best route over this irregular stretch of whitewater. The guides consulted with each other while pointing to spots in the river. Our guide reported back: "We will start on the right side of the first drop, then charge hard to the left because that large back-rolling wave will stall us out if we don't hit it hard. If we make it through that okay, just listen to me for further commands."

What do you mean *if* we make it? This was May 29th. We were about to navigate on my 50th birthday, the most revered stretch of water on the Colorado River. The adrenaline rushed through my veins. What better way to celebrate this milestone in my life? But I didn't want this to be my last birthday either.

In my opinion, the most intense part of river rafting isn't when you're in the whitewater itself, but in those moments when you're drifting toward the waiting caldron. Your pulse quickens as the roar of the rapids intensifies, but you still cannot see what is about to engulf you. Crazier still is when you are only a few feet away and you see this spot where the river drops out of sight. Now that gets your attention! At the point of no return, you get your first paralyzing glimpse of this chaotic scene into which you are about to be launched—ready or not.

Rumbling like thunder, the sound of Lava Falls was so overpowering we *felt* the vibration bouncing off the canyon walls. We barely heard our guide screaming over the noise, "Hard left! Power forward! Dig in! Harder!"

Before we knew it the massive back-rolling wall of water we had scouted earlier heaped up and towered over us. Our raft entered what looked like gaping jaws as we slammed into the teeth of this angry tsunami. Instantly we disappeared, buried by an avalanche of water. For a scary few moments we stalled out inside the churning tempest. Like sitting under a waterfall, staying in the raft was difficult and paddling seemed pointless.

Completely swamped, our raft and crew somehow emerged from the tumult looking like we'd been drinking from a fire hose. Only after we were able to catch our breath did we find out that one of our paddlers had fallen out of the raft, but in the chaos and noise no one heard her scream. Fortunately our vigilant river guide reached down, grabbed her life vest and hauled her back on board in a matter of seconds.

After successfully navigating a rapid, we'd always follow protocol by raising our paddles in the air with a shout, then smacking them in the water with a spirit of jubilation. However, our paddle-smacking after escaping Lava Falls was more somber, more reverent—almost worshipful. The river had instilled a sense of awe within us.

• • • • •

One can understand why people are drawn to worshiping nature. When engulfed by a natural wonder like the Grand Canyon, you can't help but look up where the towering rim of the canyon meets the blue sky and feel like you've been swallowed up by grandeur. Towering mountains, imposing rivers and engulfing oceans serve as eye-opening reminders that there are forces more powerful than human beings in the universe. These superlative icons of nature command our respect and warrant our reverence.

And yet, these symbols of impressive stature are not the grandest or greatest of all. All of nature points to One who is greater, the One who is transcendent over the material world. Higher than the highest peak, deeper than the deepest chasm, stronger that the strongest force in the natural order is the Grand Designer of all that is. The God who caused all that exists to come into being evokes our respect, our reverence, and our worship as supreme Lord and magnificent Creator.

However, acknowledging that God deserves our worship because he is greater than the Grand Canyon isn't going far enough. We must know what makes God superior to a river, mountain or ocean—even beyond the fact that he is the Creator of every awe-inspiring wonder in the cosmos. What elevates God above the natural world is that God is a person—a living, eternal, perfect being. This is what sets God apart.

Infinitely more complex than a cosmic force of nature, God is a person—a person who thinks, acts, creates, responds, and loves. God is not only imposing like a mountain, he is personal like a friend. When we worship God, he is our admiring audience who responds to us in ways a mountain, river, or ocean cannot. And what God did to reveal his personal nature became the most supreme act God ever accomplished on behalf of the human race. Wonder of wonders, God visited our world as a living, breathing human being. God became a man, and his name was Jesus.

Jesus makes God personal, approachable, relational. While Jesus is the same God who has the power to send thunder and lightning (Exodus 20:18, 19), he is also the One who welcomes children into his arms and blesses them (Mark 10:16). The God who transcends the heavens is also the One who descends to earth, inviting us into an intimate relationship with him. The prophet states this truth so eloquently: *"For this is what the high and exalted One says—he who lives forever, whose name is holy: 'I live in a high and holy place, but also with the one who is contrite and lowly in spirit, to revive the spirit of the lowly and to revive the heart of the contrite."* (Isaiah 57:15)

Sometimes life is as overwhelming as a towering mountain or a churning river. Sometimes it seems that God has left us in the bottom of a canyon and it is beyond our ability to find him. But the One who is above and beyond us also draws near to the humble, reviving the spirit of those who are weak and in need of his strength.

One of the most intimate and familiar scenes in the Bible is portrayed in paintings, sculptures and reenactments of the Last Supper. The twelve disciples are reclining around a table with Jesus the evening before his crucifixion. And Jesus makes the troubling announcement that one of the twelve would betray him. Here is where the scriptures reveal one of the most tender moments ever shared between Jesus and his friends.

There is a disciple who is leaning on Jesus' chest. Put yourself there if you can. Your Messiah, your Savior, the One whom Peter identified as *"...the Messiah, the Son of the living God,"* (Matthew 16:16) has just stated that one among you is a betrayer. And the disciple resting his head on Jesus' chest, later identified as John, asks, *"Lord, who is it?"* (John 13:25). The tone in his voice was not accusatory but one of sadness, empathy, and passion. More like, *Lord, this cannot be. May it not be so. I want this night to last forever. It feels so safe to be here by your side. Please do not leave us.*

But Jesus had to go to the cross for his friends and for us. Because he suffered and died we know that God indentifies with our pain and mortality. God also knows what it means to be betrayed and condemned. This is important because we do not always need a God who towers above us. We often need a God who understands—One who is able to draw near and bind up our wounds. What we need most in this life is a Savior, a Deliverer, a Lover of our souls.

Our God is the high and lofty One—but he is also the One who descends to comfort and to save. God is big enough to impress us, but becomes small enough to caress us. And this is why he is worthy of our worship and praise. May this move us, as it did the Psalmist, to cry out to our great God and compassionate Savior:

"God is our refuge and strength,
an ever-present help in trouble.
Therefore we will not fear,
though the earth give way,
and the mountains fall into the heart of the sea...
Be still, and know that I am God;
I will be exalted among the nations,
I will be exalted in the earth.
The Lord Almighty is with us,
the God of Jacob is our fortress."
(Psalm 46:1, 2, 10, 11)

The God who transcends also has ways to draw near to you no matter where you are or what you are going through. Sometimes you just have to pay attention. When you recognize his presence, you may find reason to smile, even break out in laughter. Why? Because the contrast between God's immensity and our puniness is as funny as you can imagine. When God laughs, he is never laughing *at* us but *with* us. I am certain that God has a sense of humor to have created people the likes of me and you! So get ready to laugh as you read the next story...

Compelled to Worship...

• Think of a time when you were in awe of the brute force of nature. Describe the emotions you felt.

- Identify a place where a natural wonder created a sense of reverence or the desire to worship.
- Think about how the natural realm reflects the characteristics of God. As you reflect on the diversity of creation, see how many parallels you can make with the attributes of God.
- If you can, identify a time when you experienced both the transcendence and the immanence of God—when God felt "high and lofty" yet "up close and personal" at the same time.
- What special attributes of God were revealed when he became a human being in the person of Jesus? Which of those characteristics means the most to you?

20 frozen underwear
Soul-Restoring Laughter

aron, have you seen my underwear anywhere?" I yelled from the next room.

"No."

"Well I've looked everywhere and can't find a single pair."

"I can't help you. Get dressed!" my son replied.

I was frantic. With a towel around my waist, and minutes away from the pre-wedding photo shoot for my Aaron and his bride, I couldn't find a fresh pair of briefs. I searched every room of my son's house where we were staying, and went through my suitcase for the third time. No luck.

Now running late, I exercised the only option that I could think of. I turned my used ones inside out, put them on, and that is what I wore to Aaron and Gretchen's wedding. It didn't feel quite right to be sliding a freshly pressed tuxedo over a day-old pair of underwear, but what was a man to do?

Not only was I attending the wedding, I happened to be the officiant! I struggled to keep my emotions under control while performing the ceremony. What a privilege to do the honors for two very special people who have brought so much joy into our lives as parents. Everyone who had a part in the service performed flawlessly and the reception turned into a party that rumbled long into the night.

I hadn't thought about my underwear until returning to our room and getting ready for bed. I was sure I had packed several pair for our trip. The mystery would remain unsolved for several days.

Upon returning from their honeymoon, Aaron went to the kitchen and opened the door to his freezer for the first time in two weeks. Instead of finding ice cream, he found a strange white object. He took it out and discovered it was a brick of frozen underwear. The briefs had evidently been soaked in water and placed in his freezer.

Aaron had no idea how this got there. Being a youth pastor, he thought maybe one of the students had pulled a prank or something. Thinking nothing more of it, he took the cotton block of ice and threw it in the trash.

A few days later, Aaron was hanging out with several of his buddies who had served as his groomsmen. While conversing, the subject of underwear came up. "So Aaron, did you remember to bring plenty of underwear on your honeymoon?" a friend asked.

"What kind of question is that? Of course. What are you talking about?"

"We were just wondering if you remembered to pack plenty of *Fruit of the Looms* for your trip to Italy."

"Why are you asking this? Yes! Ok? I brought plenty of…"

Aaron paused for a moment and then said, "Wait a minute… We came home from our honeymoon and I found some frozen underwear in my freezer. Did you guys have something to do with that?"

"Maybe!" One of the guys started snickering and pretty soon all of them had big grins on their faces.

"I fail to find the humor in this. Whose underwear did you put in there?" Aaron asked.

"You mean it wasn't yours?"

"No. Of course not. I don't wear 'tighty whities'— I wear boxers. You guys should know that. They weren't mine."

"But we took them out of your suitcase."

"No you didn't. My underwear were still in my…"

Aaron made another pause in mid-sentence as he remembered that his wasn't the only suitcase in the house on the day of the wedding. "Oh boy…I need to make a phone call."

I picked up his incoming call. "Hey Aaron!"

"Hey Dad, how are you doing?"

"Great! Good to hear from you. What's up?"

"Well, remember when you were huffing and puffing around my house looking for your underwear the day of my wedding?"

"I certainly do. Why do you ask?"

"Well, the crazy thing is that my groomsmen just asked me about it."

"Why would they ask you about that?"

"Because they went into the house on the day of the wedding and stole some underwear out of a suitcase they assumed was mine. I'm guessing those belonged to you!"

"What? I can't believe it! Of all the indecencies! Did you know I had no clean underwear to wear at your wedding?"

Aaron laughed. "Sorry about that Dad. If you want them back, they are melting in the bottom of my trash can."

I didn't know what to say to that. For a while I tried to be mad, but it wasn't long before I was laughing with my son over a practical joke that turned out better than the original design.

• • • • •

A common misperception about being a Christian is that the more serious you get about God the less fun you will have. The impression I get from some people is the more you look and act like a monk, the closer to God you must be. I sometimes think this is why some Christians look like they've been weaned on pickle juice or baptized in lemon juice. I sometimes want to say: *If you have the joy of the Lord in your heart, could you please inform your face?*

My wife and I attended an open-air concert at one of our local vineyards last summer. As we walked toward the elegant grounds where seats and stage were set up on the expansive lawn, an attendant handed us a half-sheet of paper that said:

Welcome to Wente Brothers Concerts at the Vineyards!
The following items are not allowed on the premises:
Food or Beverages, Cameras, Video Equipment, Radios,
Tape Recorders, Pets, Ice Chests and Coolers, Folding Chairs,
Tailgating, Cigars, Tobacco Pipes. Thank you for coming!
We hope you enjoy the evening!

I turned to my wife and said, "I don't think they want us to have any fun here." I was just kidding of course. But this is what people often do with religion. Those in charge give people a list of all the things they are not allowed to do and then say, "Welcome to the fellowship, and here are the rules. Pay attention to the 'do's and don'ts' and you'll fit in just fine."

Jesus never did that to people. When I officiate at a wedding, I sometimes reflect on the fun Jesus must have had when he performed his very first miracle—the day he turned water into wine. They had run out of wine at the wedding Jesus was attending, and so he took care of the problem:

> "*Nearby stood six stone water jars, the kind used by the Jews for ceremonial washing, each holding from twenty to thirty gallons. Jesus said to the servants, 'Fill the jars with water'; so they filled them to the brim. Then he told them, 'Now draw some out and take it to the master of the banquet.'*
>
> "*They did so, and the master of the banquet tasted the water that had been turned into wine. He did not realize where it had come from, though the servants who had drawn the water knew. Then he called the bridegroom aside and said, 'Everyone brings out the choice wine first and then the cheaper wine after the guests have had too much to drink; but you have saved the best till now.'*" (John 2:6-10)

One hundred and fifty gallons of water turned into one hundred and fifty gallons of wine! Not cheap stuff either. This wine tasted like a special vintage aged in French oak barrels for years and had been uncorked at just the right time. This "Jesus Wine" was far superior to the "choice wine" that was offered to the guests that day. I can only imagine that this party went long into the night and would be talked about for years to come.

What's intriguing is that Jesus made a choice to solve a problem that wasn't a serious matter at all. Unlike other miracles where matters of life and death were at stake, running out of wine wasn't a crisis of epic proportion. It could even be argued that since the people already had plenty to drink, there was good reason to simply call it a night. So why did he do it?

Certainly this miracle was one of many signs he gave to his closest followers to help convince them of his divine nature. But what Jesus did also contributed to the happiness and pleasure the people were enjoying. In a behind the scenes sort of way, Jesus added his toast to the merriment going on. What is very clear about Jesus' actions is that he wasn't sending a message that said: *Knock it off—you're having too much fun.*

If there was ever an endorsement by God that enjoying life is no sin, turning water into wine at a wedding feast was it. Even if you do not enjoy wine or do not drink it for personal reasons, the principle here cannot be ignored. Instead of preaching a sermon against the dangers of levity, Jesus enhanced the atmosphere of amusement and good cheer. The deeper truth is that happiness and pleasure have their source in God himself. Laughter is one of God's own inventions given as a gift to lighten our burdens and to lessen the sorrows of life.

This is not to say that having fun is the ultimate pursuit or the greatest purpose for living. But enjoying God is! Delightful, cascading joy flows from the heart of God. The more we get to know him, the more we realize that God is a happy God. As our lives absorb more of his life, we become happier people. Relationships go deeper, love runs thicker, generosity grows larger, and belly laughs echo louder because the joy runs deep.

For this we were born, to find in God the kind of satisfaction we all want and are looking for. The biggest surprise for many of us is that God's life is as emancipating as it is exhilarating. God's grand design for our lives is one of liberation from whatever is holding us back from becoming all we were meant to be. In other words, Jesus came to set us free not to tie us down. We are reminded of Jesus' own words, reflecting the purpose of why he came into this world: "I have come that they may have life and have it to the full." (John 10:10b)

Ironically, as we take God more seriously and ourselves less seriously, joy intensifies and laughter resounds more and more. Yes, God gives us permission to laugh and loves it when his smile meets ours. No matter what you are going through this day, I encourage you to find that place in your soul where you and God are smiling, chuckling and embracing—it's the only way to live.

Soul-Restoring Laughter...
- What's the most fun you've ever had? What made you laugh long and hard?
- Do you have a hard time equating God with fun or pleasure? Why or why not?
- Do you see God as happy or harsh? Explain.
- What insights about God does the "water into wine" incident reveal to you, if any?
- What might "enjoying God" look like in your everyday life?

21 circus circus
Unrestricted Freedom

On a sub-zero February morning, my wife and I loaded our twenty-two-foot *Ryder* truck with our three kids, a dog, and everything we owned, towing a twelve-foot Shasta camper trailer, followed by a full-size family station wagon. We had enough space for everything—except for our picnic table which we strapped to the back of the truck. We looked like something out of *The Grapes of Wrath* as our mini-caravan rolled in a westward direction.

We were leaving behind a wonderful church family in Wisconsin to follow a prompting from God to launch a new church in the San Francisco Bay area. We began this week-long journey of 2200 miles in the dead of winter. I wouldn't recommend this trip to anyone.

The first mishap took place when I made a wrong turn on an Illinois Interstate taking us south toward Chicago instead of west toward Omaha. The next day a fifty-mile-per-hour crosswind blasted us in Nebraska making the truck lean at an angle down Interstate 80. Relieved to exit Nebraska, a blizzard greeted us in Wyoming. Dumping two feet of snow, the storm halted all forward progress in Laramie. When we were allowed back on the highway, a stiff sub-zero wind slammed us head-on where it was pedal-to-the-metal with a top speed of thirty-five miles-per-hour through the Rocky Mountains.

But the worst incident happened in Salt Lake City where the truck separated from the car in heavy traffic. I had lost my wife. This was the late 80's when there were no cell phones. Pulling off at a random exit, I sat there watching the minutes tick by, praying that God would help us find each other. I couldn't believe my eyes when I spotted a maroon station wagon coming down the exit ramp. I got out and waved my arms. How we reunited is a mystery. But as we hugged each other with teary eyes, we were convinced that God was directing our paths.

Reno, Nevada was the last stop in our journey west. I pulled up to a gas station and asked the attendant if he could recommend a nice, moderately priced, family-type motel in the area. "Sure, that's easy. The cheapest place in town right now is *Circus Circus* at twenty-two dollars per night. Your kids will love it."

"OK, how do we get there?" He gave me instructions that took us into downtown Reno. *Circus Circus* turned out to be a huge casino-hotel that featured ongoing circus acts inside. I'll never forget the look on the valet's face as I pulled up to the glitzy entrance in our *Ryder* truck, towing the Shasta camper trailer, followed by our rust-covered car.

"We're part of the circus," I said. "Where should we park?"

"Where are you from?"

"Wisconsin."

"That explains it."

He stared at our unsightly entourage. "You can't park here, but there's a big gravel parking lot a half-mile down the street. You can park there."

Now that's convenient, I thought. A wife, three kids, a dog, suitcases, an ice chest, and a half-mile walk—perfect! But the twenty-two-dollars-a-night deal was stuck in my mind, and it was getting late. We drove down there, parked in this pitch black gravel parking lot, and walked away thinking we'd get ripped off for sure.

At eight o'clock that night, after dragging everything up the street, we finally reached the hotel counter at *Circus Circus*—only to be told that this double-high-rise hotel with hundreds of rooms was booked solid! I stared at the woman behind the front desk in disbelief. The kids were cranky and there was no way we were hiking back down to that parking lot.

"Don't worry sir, the *Shamrock Hotel* next door will honor our rates," said the receptionist. "Would you like me to call them for you?"

"Fine," I said. With protests from our tired children, we walked out of the front entrance of *Circus Circus*, made our way to the *Shamrock* and checked in. As we entered our room, I immediately realized why the *Shamrock* wasn't booked solid. "Creepy" best described the atmosphere that reeked of stale cigarette smoke. But for only a quarter, our lumpy queen-sized mattress would vibrate. Such a deal!

Arriving in California the next day, we opened our suitcases and could smell the *Shamrock Hotel*. While unloading our belongings into a rental house in a strange town among strange people, we began wondering what we were doing here. Those words of warning from family and friends back east began to loom large. We heard things like: "California? Why would you go there? That's where there are earthquakes, wildfires, mudslides, and the people there are not normal. Why would you bring your family to such a place?"

Those early days were not easy and doubts often crept in. One thing I had no doubt about—God would have to loom larger than our challenges in order for us to establish a new church in this part of the world. Thankfully, God did.

• • • • •

I spent several days doing a door-to-door survey because I was interested to find out why such a small percentage of bay area people attended church. Five main reasons came up over and over.

"It's not worth my time," was the most common. Eight out of ten people expressed this, saying the church did not offer them enough value. I heard comments such as: *"I know what goes on there…Church is boring…I have more important things to do…Been there, done that."*

A second objection to attending church was: *"I don't need to go to church to be a good person."* People expressed this by saying things like: *"I can worship God on my own…I have my own ways of connecting with God…I am not a fan of organized religion."*

A third reason: *"The sermons are irrelevant to my life."* They didn't know they were talking to a pastor when they said: *"Pastors and priests are great at talking about subjects no one cares about… They need to speak about issues I face in my everyday life."*

A fourth objection to church attendance was: *"The church is full of hypocrites."* Typical statements were: *"Christians don't practice what they preach…Church people are judgmental…I would not fit in because I have done some bad things."*

Finally, people commented that: *"The church is always asking for money."* Their statements about money represented experiences they had with a particular church or a perception of church they assumed to be true.

After this bit of research, I knew we had our work cut out for us. The church we planned to start needed to be relevant, not boring, worth people's time, authentic, and sensitive about the issue of money. We'd need to accept people for who they are and extend heaps of mercy and grace upon them. Finally, I thought a band would be better than a choir—but other than that, I had no idea what I was doing.

Thankfully, God did. We launched our new church and it began to grow rapidly. I tried to make my sermons simple and relevant to modern life. When I failed to do that, people were gracious. I didn't know, for example, that my story about picking up "road kill" would get such mixed reviews. I explained to my California audience how poor we were in my first church in northern Minnesota, and that I was on the game warden's call list whenever a deer got killed on the county road. We were always happy to get the fresh meat. After revealing that story, I learned to be more culturally sensitive.

We raised some eyebrows the Sunday morning I rode my *Harley Davidson* onto the stage while we blasted the song *Born To Be Wild* from the speakers. And we had some fun the day I rode an *ATV* around the sanctuary to complement a Country Western theme. We've never been afraid to take risks and do the unexpected in a Sunday service. But what I love most about *CrossWinds Church* is its reputation as a place where people are free to come as they are and explore a relationship with the God who loves them. Even guys who pick up road-kill are accepted!

Perhaps you have not walked through the door of a church in years, except perhaps for Christmas and Easter. You may have reasons for not attending similar to the objections I found in my neighborhood survey. Granted, the church is often its own worst enemy. We hear about the church scandals, the clergy caught up in immoral behavior, and the church caring more about its institutions and traditions than the people entrusted to its care. Add to this the history of the church where war, bloodshed and suffering were inflicted in God's name. Clearly the Christian church has not always represented Christ well.

These are just a few of the reasons why you may have trouble seeing the church as a place where you can find God or receive help for your problems. But there are good churches all across America that are putting the needs of people first, making a huge difference in their communities, and reflecting Jesus' life and teachings authentically. Sometimes you need to do some searching to find one of these Christian communities in your area, but you can do it.

Maybe you are one who shares the view of many non-churchgoers: *I can worship God on my own—I don't need a church to do that.* Actually there is truth to this statement. Many of the stories in this book describe my own worship experiences and times of prayer in places other than church. But consider the power in a community coming together for the same unified purpose— to worship God and to encourage each other in their spiritual journeys. There is strength, energy, support, insight, and kindness that can be felt and received when a Jesus-centered community gathers and prays. This is when God shows up, draws near, and makes himself known in surprising ways.

If you are concerned that attending church or getting too serious about religion will diminish your freedom or take away what you enjoy, this is not what Jesus lived or taught at all. He came to establish a relationship with us, not to institute a religion. Our world reflects a joyful Creator who invites us to enjoy life and live it to the full. I can assure you that your sense of freedom will increase as your intimacy with God grows. Living God's life is an emancipating experience.

A relationship with God is about freeing us from the sin patterns that become a life-stealing burden. When entrapments such as anger, bitterness, cynicism, arrogance and fear are replaced with love, joy, peace, hope, mercy and grace, our lives are set free. It's never too late to become the person you've always wanted to be. A grace-filled, Christ-centered church can be the best way for you to discover God's liberating design for your life.

So, if you really want to go against the grain by doing something widely unpopular, highly countercultural, and quite courageous—become part of a good local church. Visit a few churches in your area before you decide which one to call 'home.' This could be the best thing that ever happened to you. And if you are already connected with a church in your community, well, I'm preaching to the choir!

Unrestricted Freedom...

- What is your religious background if any? How did your past experience with religion or church affect you?
- Do you generally have a favorable view or an unfavorable view of churches? Explain where your perspective comes from.

- Why do you think most people do not attend church these days? What do you think could be done to make attending church more appealing?
- If you are a Christian, can you describe ways in which Jesus has liberated your life? What does it mean when we say that "Christ has set us free?"
- If you are a member of a local church family, express how you became connected with that church and the difference this has made in your life.

22

whitney
Ultimate Happiness

"Jeff, you have the tent, right? I have one if you don't."

"No worries John. I just bought a new two man tent. We're good—no need to carry two tents up there."

I should've asked him to show me the tent but there seemed no need to do that. Being an experienced climber, I trusted his judgment when it came to equipment and planning. To his credit, Jeff has hiked the sixteen-mile round trip from Yosemite Valley to the top of Half Dome twenty-five years in a row. I've done it with him twice. The 4500-foot elevation gain will test your stamina, but what makes the climb unique is scaling up and down the cable ladder bolted into the granite wall on Half Dome's back side. This last 400 feet of vertical is where many climbers look up, become intimidated, bail out, and fail to see the stunning view of Yosemite Valley from the top of the Dome.

For years we had talked about climbing Mount Whitney, the tallest peak in the contiguous United States at 14,497 feet. It was time to act. Five of us formed the initial group of hikers, but one by one people dropped out with lame excuses for not being able to go. Jeff and I were the only two left standing at the Whitney Portal trailhead on a beautiful July morning.

"They don't know what they are missing," said Jeff about our absent friends.

"Yeah, I'd much rather be working today like they are." After that sarcastic comment, we kicked up our heels toward base camp at 11,000 feet. There we'd spend the night acclimating to the altitude, summit the following morning, and then climb back down to the trail head before nightfall.

We knew the temperature would drop as we gained altitude but were surprised to find a thick snowpack at base camp with solid ice blanketing the pond nearby. As the sun set, a chill in the air caused us to scramble for jackets. With a temperature of ninety degrees in the valley below, it was hard to imagine that temperatures would drop below zero that night. Little did we know how unprepared we were until Jeff decided it was time to set up his new tent.

If it were not for the ominous signs of a very cold night descending upon us, the little red diamond-shaped tent sitting on a bed of snow would have been comical. "I thought you bought a two-man tent."

"I did," said Jeff. "It says *5x6 Two Man Tent* right here on the label."

"Looks like a half-man tent to me. Try laying down in there."

Jeff crawled in and could not stretch out his legs. No wonder—the tent was about four feet long by four feet wide.

The man had bought a kid's tent designed for eight-year-old sleepovers in the backyard!

"Where am I supposed to sleep?" I asked.

"Oh, you can fit—you may have to stick your legs out the door."

I was not laughing. "How much did you pay for this thing?" He was embarrassed to admit that he paid $19.99 at Wal-Mart.

He tried to do the Christian thing by half-heartedly suggesting that I sleep in the tent while he slept outside. Just the opposite happened. I stretched out a ground tarp on the snow bank, unpacked my sleeping bag rated for thirty-two degrees, and put on every stitch of clothing I had with me. At first it was not so bad lying in the open air, mesmerized by the brilliance of the stars and constellations. I soon fell asleep.

At midnight a cold wind awakened me. I tried wrapping the tarp around my sleeping bag as a wind block. But after drifting in and out of sleep, I woke at 3 AM shivering. I lay there trying not to think angry thoughts about Jeff which was difficult. By 4 AM I gave up on sleeping, got up, started the gas burner and made coffee. That helped warm me a little.

I sat huddled against a rock till about 5:30 AM. By then I was done listening to Jeff snoring so I woke him up and told him it was time to eat breakfast and start hiking. "That was the coldest, windiest, nosiest nights I've ever experienced in the mountains," he said.

"At least you were in a tent." I kept from making further comments because what I was thinking of saying wasn't very nice.

The blood began circulating and warming our extremities as we scrambled up the first sharp incline. The saw toothed Sierra Crest became a cathedral of light as the rising sun cast soft hues followed by shimmering streaks across the face of giant granite walls.

Walking up craggy inclines and over narrow ridges, we arrived at the summit in glorious California sunshine. The 360 degree panorama took in vast slices of the Sierra Nevada Mountain range that included peaks, valleys, lakes and deserts. Jeff and I stood arm-in-arm on the geological marker with big grins, pumping our fists into the thin air.

What we had suffered the night before now seemed like a distant memory. I knew that without Jeff's companionship we would not be standing on this pinnacle of accomplishment. I was grateful for him. Nothing could steal the light-headed joy we experienced in that moment of euphoric celebration. While dancing around on the highest peak we'd ever been on in our lives, heaven felt closer. Life felt larger.

On our way back down the mountain Jeff said, "Let's do this again next year."

"Maybe," I replied. "But if we do, I'll bring the tent."

• • • • •

Don't blink… That was eight years ago. I'm now sixty-two. Jeff is fifty-six. I got a call from him a few months ago. The trembling in his voice told me something was wrong. "John, do you have a few minutes?"

"Sure. What's going on?"

"You aren't going to believe this because I can hardly believe this. But for the past few months I've had all this weird stuff going on with me. It started out with a dizzy, confused feeling—like I was having an out-of-body experience just walking around. Then my ears started ringing loudly, and some body parts were swelling up. I began losing weight, strength and energy levels.

"I tried to hide it from my staff but overheard one of them saying I wasn't on top of my game—which was true. My symptoms baffled my doctors. I had brain scans, spinal fluid taps, over fifty blood tests, but the diagnosis was inconclusive. For months I prayed and cried at night asking God to heal me or take me. I was miserable.

"Finally the classic symptoms of a well know disease began revealing themselves. One night I couldn't write the number 3. My arm stopped swinging when I walked. I couldn't write my own signature, and my face became very non-expressive.

"John, I found out that I have Parkinson's disease—at fifty-five years old. I am so confused by this. But I just wanted you to know."

"Wow Jeff. Like you said—this is hard to believe. I am so sorry. My heart goes out to you brother. I can only begin to imagine how confusing this is for you right now. Is there any way I can help you with anything?"

"Just pray—pray for me and my wife. And I would appreciate you keeping this confidential for now. This raises so many uncertainties about the future for me, and for my wife, and my business. Photography and Parkinson's don't seem to be very compatible so I prefer that my clients don't find out about this prematurely. I need to keep working as long as I can."

"I understand my friend. I'll be praying, and let's keep in touch."

"Thanks. I'd be dishonest not to admit that I'm bewildered and worried about this. I have no idea what this means. And I wonder if I'll ever be able to climb again."

After saying good-bye, I slumped back in my chair wanting to believe the conversation I just had was an illusion. Whenever I think of Jeff, mountaintop experiences come to mind. What I just heard did not fit that picture. He was always happiest in high places. How would he cope with this new low place that would take him into unfamiliar and uninviting territory?

Thankfully, the adventurous, never-say-die spirit within my friend has not been snuffed out. As weeks turned into months, Jeff began climbing in a different way—he is gaining elevation mentally, emotionally and spiritually. While admitting some embarrassment about having this disease, and that he hated the idea of getting pity from his family and friends, he also said this: "I do know there will be some kind of good that comes out of this. I have seen *Romans 8:28* played out so many times in my life. And I see God's hand in a lot of things happening right now."

Romans 8:28 says, *"And we know that in all things God works for the good of those who love him, who have been called according to his purpose."* Jeff believed that and decided to live in the assurance of that promise. He didn't know what God had in mind, but he was choosing to believe that something bigger than Parkinson's disease would come of this.

What inspired me was the new perspective my friend had about life. He said, "I've gotten over most of the sadness and feel like I am on a mission now. I feel this passion welling up in me. I want this next part of my life to be very significant."

And then he said something that will always stick with me: "I want to hit the tape hard and finish strong. No rocking chairs, no take it easy attitude."

I thought to myself: *That's the Jeff I know and love!* "I want to hit the tape hard and finish strong!" Hum…Could it be that this setback was causing him to throttle forward? I think so. He's decided he's not finished. Listen to this:

"I was driving in my car today and praying: *God, show me my calling. Show me what you want me to do in the time I have left.*

"I've worked hard the past thirty-one years of my life, and the hard work has paid off pretty well. Ah, but this next part of my life—that's where I want to *kick butt!*

"I have this vision that when I meet the Lord he will have a grin on his face, a grin of pride. We will pound fists and 'blow it up!' And we will hug for a long time, and find in that embrace a happiness that cannot be described."

When he said that my mind went back to the top of Mount Whitney where Jeff and I hugged and pumped our fists in the air. I captured a glimpse of this vision he was describing—a vision of rapture on earth that ascended to heaven itself because God's presence was so real.

I also remembered something he said after that sleepless night on the mountain, followed by the hike up and back down all in the same day. We sat down at trails end exhausted—everything was sore. As we examined our hard-earned calluses, Jeff said, "You know, the suffering kind of makes this more special, doesn't it? It's weird how that works. We wouldn't be nearly as happy as we are right now if it didn't hurt—because the pain reminds you that you accomplished something significant, and that it wasn't easy."

My throat was too parched to respond. I nodded my head and smiled. He was articulating a long-held conviction of my own— that how we seek to attain happiness is often misguided. When happiness becomes the goal, we naturally think that difficulty, pain or trouble is what is to be avoided. But we will never arrive at the mountain's summit, nor find the deep level of enjoyment that God has for us until we put on the hiking boots, and face whatever the mountain wants to throw in our path.

If there was a guiding life principle that would summarize what I've sought to portray in this book, it's this: *The #1 principle in life is the pursuit of God and God's life—and when we keep that pursuit #1, happiness will follow.* When more of God becomes the cause in your life, happiness is the effect.

However, when we turn that principle around by pursuing happiness first, and hope God will bless that pursuit, or that God will come along for the ride, or even worse, get out of the way—this always results in either disappointment or disaster. If you're skeptical about the idea that pursuing God will lead to happiness because when you think of God, *happy* is not the first adjective that comes to mind, then there is something about who God is that we must always remember.

This is what we must know about God's nature: *God is a happy God. God's life is a happy life. And to live God's life means sharing in his happiness.* If this is a new thought for you—that God is a happy Being, and that a relationship with him means entering into his happiness—then let's stop and think about why this wouldn't be true.

The Bible tells us that God's life and the essence of who God is consists of love, joy, peace, beauty and pleasure. Think about the smile on God's face and the bliss he experienced after completing each act of creation. After creating the stars and galaxies, the oceans and mountain peaks, the fish, birds and animals, he saw the magnificence of his universe and was delighted in its splendor. And then he fashioned human beings in his own likeness—men and women designed to love as God loves, and to share in the happiness of enjoying his wonderful creation. Just as God was pleased and satisfied with the work he had done, so he was happy to invite us to share in his good pleasure.

Allow me to give you permission to play God for a minute. Put yourself in his sovereign position and think about what an omniscient, omnipresent God is privileged to see and experience every moment from every possible point of view. He simultaneously sees every snow-covered mountain range, every palm-covered beach, every waterfall, every coral reef, every multi-colored bird in the jungle, every calving glacier, every sunrise and sunset, every meteor shower and galactic explosion throughout the universe. We can only imagine that what God experiences must cause great tidal waves of joy to wash over his being all the time.

If what I have just described is even close to who God is and what he experiences, then why wouldn't we want to be in hot pursuit of God and the happiness found in him? Why would we settle for anything less than what we were created for? The difference maker is to keep the pursuit of God as the #1 priority in our lives—keep that straight and then watch what happens next.

Before I close this chapter, I will remind you of something that may sound paradoxical in light of what was just expressed. We must remember that God's #1 priority for our lives is not to make us happy. *God's #1 priority is to love us—not to make us happy.* God has committed himself to love you when you are sad, mad, confused or frightened—even when you are being tested or disciplined—God is committed to walk though that with you. And happiness is the by-product of realizing God's presence with you.

We cannot escape the fact that we live in a world where we suffer grief and hardship of many kinds. There will be tears, there will be sorrow, there will be anguish—and we must remember that this is normal. When life hits you with a disease that you never saw coming, you have to remember that God hasn't abandoned you. Just because you are not feeling happy doesn't mean that God is not there or that he doesn't care.

God has promised he will love us through any situation—but he never said it would be easy. The suffering we must endure in this life may be as small as calluses on our feet or as huge as

Parkinson's that wracks our bodies. In either case, God is able to provide the strength enabling us to declare: *I want to hit the tape hard and finish strong!*

And when you cross the finish line, you'll look back and perhaps see how the pain made the experience more special—you'll know you've accomplished something significant, and that it wasn't easy. Ironically, you may find this elevates your happiness and joy in this life. And best of all, you'll discover that you're living life the way it was meant to be lived.

Ultimate Happiness...

- What was the most difficult hike or climb you've ever accomplished? How was the degree of difficulty rewarded by the level of accomplishment you felt?
- In what ways have you sought to find happiness? What do you think of the premise that if we keep God as our #1 pursuit, happiness will follow?
- Does it make sense to you that God is a happy God? What are some obstacles that get in the way of enjoying God and his creation?
- What "mountain" may God be calling you to climb while you still have time?
- In what specific way do you desire to *hit the tape hard and finish strong?*

23

friendly fire
Surprising Peace

'm shot!" my brother Bob screamed.

Ignoring his cry I yelled, "Shoot! Shoot!"

Beating wings and nervous quacks from a dozen plump Canadian Mallards could be heard a few feet in front of us. And then from our brushy hiding spot we saw them rising up in perfect shooting range. But before we could fire a shot, we were hit by pellets coming from other guns blazing away just a few yards from where we sat. I had always wondered what it felt like to be on the receiving end of incoming fire power—now I knew.

Everything happened so quickly—the rising ducks, the distant shots, the sting of BB-sized buckshot hitting us in the legs, arms and face. Out of pure instinct I gave the command to shoot, knowing we had mere seconds before the mallards would be out of range and long gone. Somehow we stood up, fired, and several mallards dropped out of the sky. We then slumped down in the bushes to assess the seriousness of our wounds.

Every fall a group of us maintained a tradition of heading up North when the frost appeared and the leaves were turning red and gold. Loaded up with canoes and backpacks full of gear we ventured into the Boundary Waters Canoe Area where lakes and streams create a vast wilderness area uniting Minnesota and Ontario. Summer-loving tourists were no longer around, and thankfully, neither were the mosquitoes. Days were spent catching Walleyed Pike and jump-shooting migrating mallards. Nights were spent around a campfire listening to the haunting cry of loons and watching the Northern Lights gyrate across the sky.

But on the first day of paddling, we came upon a familiar spot in a stream that flowed through a large marshy area—a perfect duck hang-out. Sure enough, we spotted some mallards 100 yards away and concocted a plan that was badly flawed. My brother and I circled around and positioned ourselves where we thought was just beyond the sitting ducks. The plan was for our two buddies to wait till we got into position before paddling down the stream. The hope was that they would get shooting as the ducks flushed and that we would get in on the shoot as the ducks flew past us.

The flaw in the plan was revealed when my brother and I found ourselves hiding in the direct line of fire of our approaching friends. As soon as the birds rose off the water, guns started booming and pellets were peppering the brush like popcorn. I had always assumed that friendly fire only happened in the military— not true! This is when Bob screamed, "John, I'm shot! I'm hit!"

Bob was to my left and protected me from most of the flying lead. The first thing I noticed was a small trickle of blood running down his face. One thing about my brother—he does not like the sight of blood, especially when it's his own. I watched his face turn pale and then break out in a cold sweat. I thought he was going to faint.

"Bob, take it easy—you're not going to die," I told him. I could have phrased that better as my comments did little to reassure him—he was swooning like a limp fish. I did a quick examination of our exposed skin and found that all of our wounds were superficial except one. One pellet had struck Bob in the eyebrow and somehow came to rest between his eyelid and eyeball. I reached up and put my finger on his eyelid and could feel the little round projectile in there. The BB had somehow glanced off the ledge of his skull and stopped short of penetrating his eye by an eyelash.

Our buddies had no idea what had happened until they found us in the bushes with Bob holding a bloody handkerchief to his face. They felt terrible, of course, and expressed their heart-felt apologies for what was an innocent mistake. We told them it wasn't their fault and wouldn't hold it against them—which was only partly true. Every year after that incident the story was retold and embellished around the campfire. In jest we'd say, "What kind of friends would fire upon their buddies in a defenseless position? You had better be watching your backsides on this trip!"

While Bob's condition was not life-threatening, we were concerned about the possibility of infection and the discomfort of having that object in such a sensitive area. So we paddled out, visited the ER in the local town, and through a simple procedure the pellet was plucked from Bob's eyelid. We then paddled back in and finished the trip. No scars were incurred—only memories about what might have happened, but didn't. And musings about what did happen gave way to expressions of gratitude to God. We had been under fire and emerged nearly unscathed.

• • • • •

While you may have never been hit by real bullets, you know what it feels like to be "under the gun." Sometimes out of nowhere there are heat-seeking projectiles bearing down on you. You may have tried to run for cover, only to find yourself hiding under the wrong bush. You're pleading for mercy, hoping for a ceasefire, but there seems to be little relief in sight. If only you could call a truce, get beyond survival mode, and restore some semblance of peace. But instead, the battle rages.

I think of the battalion of marines who had been in the trenches for several days. Their job was to hold down the front line by resisting any advance from the enemy. On a wet, cold evening when morale was sinking, the chaplain radioed one of the marines and said, "Soldier, I am praying that God will be with you and strengthen you."

The young marine responded, "Thank you sir, but God isn't in this foxhole."

Suddenly a mortar shell screamed through the air and exploded a few feet away from where the marine was hiding. Quickly he radioed the chaplain and said, "Correction sir! God just dropped in!"

When we're facing the intense pressure of being under fire, it may appear that God has either abandoned us or is just using us for target practice. But if we would take a closer look, sometimes it is simply "friendly fire" that is not designed to maim, kill or destroy—but to let us know that where we're hiding is not a safe place. It may be that the plan we've concocted is a flawed one and God is warning us to abandon this self-directed path that is riddled with land mines.

In recent months, I have been on a personal quest that I think you may be interested in exploring with me. Simply stated, I've been on a quest for personal peace. It began with a six month sabbatical leave from my work at the church after nearly twenty-five years of ministry as the lead pastor. This was a wonderful gift of time and should have been one of the most enjoyable, care-free, mind-cleansing seasons of my adult life. To some extent it was, but I was perplexed over my inability to be at peace much of the time. Often I'd find myself obsessing over problems at church that were no longer mine to solve or be concerned about.

Even more upsetting was the mental energy spent on what I call "replaying the tapes" in my head—replaying past skirmishes with people where I was wounded due to misunderstanding, criticism or betrayal. These were situations that I had given back to God and had practiced forgiveness a long time ago. And yet, when my mind should have been at rest and my soul at peace, I would find my idle thoughts drifting down those same old paths. This was not only a waste of time but wasn't contributing to my mental or spiritual health.

I became so frustrated over what I labeled as my "mental clutter" that I poured out my heart to God in prayer about this. I began asking God to clear my mind of the muddle, keep me from going back to the memory bank, and stop the tiring business of opening up old wounds. This is serious business because an unbridled mind can be where the evil one can do what he does best—suck the life, joy, and peace right out of our lives. As opposed to friendly fire, this is where the howitzer of enemy fire can knock us on our backsides by convincing us to keep living in the past. And this is the biggest waste of time and energy we could ever manage to fabricate as human beings.

After months of praying for peace, and realizing that someone can throw a grenade in your foxhole at any moment, destroying any figment of tranquility you thought you had—I began to learn something. Peace is mainly a matter of what is going on between our ears. As long as there is too much "interior noise" or "cerebral static" there will be no semblance of the peace we are searching for. While I am not a genius at this, I can tell you that some mental discipline is required here.

The Apostle Paul did not take this battle of the mind lightly. He referred to it as "waging war." Here is how he describes the conflict: *"For though we live in the world, we do not wage war as the world does. The weapons we fight with are not the weapons of the world. On the contrary, they have divine power to demolish strongholds. We demolish arguments and every pretension that sets itself up against the knowledge of God, and we take captive every thought to make it obedient to Christ."* (II Corinthians 10:3-5)

Paul acknowledges that we are fighting a battle but the way we fight it is far different from the way the nations of the world wage war. This is not a type of combat involving tanks, fighter jets, missiles and guns. It is rather a spiritual and mental battle involving divine power teaming up with human resistance. The fortifications of mental clutter, spiritual confusion and emotional scarring can be beaten and overcome. What is required is a decisive, intentional decision each and every day to "take captive every thought and make it obedient to Christ". This daily exercise includes conscious discipline of our minds, disallowing them to spin off into unchecked defeatist thinking. The additional action in winning the battle of the mind is the persistent yielding of control to our Commander-in-Chief, Jesus Christ. We must focus our attention to the directives of the Lord our God and ask him to transform our thinking to be more like his own.

In terms of further human action, I recommend hanging around people who seem to have a lot of peace and joy in their lives—this can be contagious. It is also beneficial to have someone in your life who has permission to confront you when you're choosing to be much more despondent and irritable than you have reason to be.

My wife is pretty good at this and will call me out when she sees me going into what she calls a "blue funk." That is her diagnosis and label of my mood when it seems like I have the weight of the world on my shoulders. A couple of months ago I was in a bad blue funk lasting much longer than was good for anyone, and I said to her, "I don't know why I'm feeling so down—I really have no reason to be."

She said, "That's right! You have no reason to be—so snap out of it!" And then she preached a brief message that she had probably heard me preach somewhere along the way. "Joy and peace is a choice—you can either choose to be happy and content or continue being a grouch. So please, either choose joy and peace or go see a shrink." In other words, practice what you preach buddy. I needed that symbolic slap in the face.

Here's the truth of the matter—Christians have every reason to be the most "at peace" people on the planet. Why? Because even when we find ourselves under fire, the Lord God serves as our greatest ally, trusted companion, and guide to safe refuge. Because God stands with us and goes before us, there's nothing to fear or dread. As people of faith, we should know and believe that it's not just us against the world. Listen to these comforting, reassuring words of Jesus to his followers: *"Peace I leave with you; my peace I give you. I do not give to you as the world gives. Do not let your hearts be troubled and do not be afraid."* (John 14:27)

Jesus offers and extends to us his peace. What kind of peace is this? Not some sort of false hope, or peace at any price, or conditional peace, or contractual peace representing a cessation of fighting. More than the offering of an olive branch, Jesus invites us into his peace—the peace of God who is never fearful, anxious, troubled or confused. This inner tranquility is the state of a soul that is calm, content, at ease and happy. While unseen on the inside, it is often revealed on the outside when someone like yourself goes through an excruciating trial or is under a severe attack and remains composed. This reveals a trust in God who is bigger than the trial and is being relied upon as the sovereign Lord of every situation.

How I pray for this peace in your life and mine. I pray for this peace to sweep over our nation and world. I'd ask you to join me by praying that people will be reconciled to God, and find a peace in their life that could have never existed otherwise. Pray that as people find God's peace, this will impact their relationships in a way that brings healing and restoration.

Finally, I pray that you will be surprised by the kind of peace that enables you to rise above the panic when all hell seems to be breaking loose around you. Maybe from the outside people see the challenges in your marriage, or see your less than perfect kids, or know about your struggling company, or your growing mound of debt, or your life-threatening illness, or all of the above—and yet what is also seen is a calmness about you. May there be evidence of an underlying peace that transcends the chaos.

May the God of peace soothe, protect and strengthen your heart, mind and soul both now and forevermore. In the strong name of Jesus, Amen!

Surprising Peace...

- Have you ever been "under fire" (either literally or figuratively) because you found yourself in the wrong place at the wrong time? What was the outcome?

- What comes to mind when you think of peace from a global or historical perspective? Why do you think attaining peace is often so illusive?
- What might it mean for you to "take captive every thought to make it obedient to Christ" as it relates to mental clutter and unhealthy thought patterns?
- Reflect on what Jesus meant when he offered us his peace. How does God's peace differ from other perceptions of what peace is?

conclusion

My eyes blinked as my head broke above the surface of the river. A backpack caught in the current quickly floated out of reach. But it wasn't the backpack or the overturned boat that concerned me. My boys. Where were my boys?

Spinning around I spotted them—two toe-heads bobbing down the river with their chins above water. "Are you ok?" I yelled.

"Yes dad!" yelling back in unison.

"Swim to the bank as hard as you can," I ordered. Though only ages 13 and 10, Aaron and Nate both swam on the community swimming team back home. Never did I think it would be in the middle of the Snake River where I'd find comfort in their ability to swim.

Swimming after them, the three of us gathered in a backwater eddy treading water. Looking into each other's faces our collective expression was that of *what just happened?* The answer? Dad wasn't paying attention—that's what happened!

Launching our drift boat below Hells Canyon Dam in Idaho, the first six miles of a planned thirty-five mile float trip went without a hitch. Stunning scenery, excellent fishing, and easily negotiated Class II rapids elicited some early thrills. But as confidence grew, vigilance became compromised. With fishing lines in the water, a Class III rapid caught us by surprise and flipped our boat.

Exiting a river entombed by canyon walls proved daunting. Living up to its name, Hells Canyon seemed hell-bent on burying us as we struggled to find a way out of there. Providentially, our boat came swirling by and we grabbed hold of this impromptu floatation device. Finding a narrow opening between boulders, we finally dragged our chilled bodies and swamped boat out of the icy water.

Wet and shivering on top of a large boulder, we were stunned—yet happy to be alive. Taking inventory, we were down to one drift boat and one water-logged back pack containing soaked sleeping bags, fishing tackle and some food. A soggy loaf of bread became fish food but we salvaged some freeze-dried meals, waterproof matches and a few camping items.

Little did we know that this mini-disaster had just saved us from what could have been a deadly tragedy. Though we didn't realize it just yet, we later agreed that this mishap was God's wake-up call to a greater impending danger. Collecting our wits, we decided to make our way down river to a camping spot just above a treacherous Class IV set of rapids called "Wild Sheep." Arriving at the campsite, we could hear the roar of Wild Sheep and see the mist rising up from the first major drop of the raging abyss.

"No way are we going over that dad!" said Aaron. He verbalized what all of us were thinking. No way were we going to risk a Class

IV when we just got dumped by a Class III. After a couple of days of camping, we caught a jet boat ride back up river to our starting point. On our way back home, the words I've repeated over and over through the years resounded in my soul: *It's good to be alive!*

There's a question I've been asking you to ponder as you've journeyed through this book: What is it that causes you to say: *It's good to be alive!* My hope is that you've developed a clearer answer to this question along with a greater resolve to pursue what makes your soul thrive.

One final word—the trip down the Snake River was yet another reminder that *life can be swept away at any time.* Because this is true, we must be diligent about living life this day because there are no guarantees about someday. Life on this earth is tenuous and uncertain. This is why I've urged you, chapter after chapter, to deepen your personal relationship with God—*in whom there is always a someday.*

Your immortal soul yearns for the eternal—for someone and something that transcends the temporary nature of earthly life. That *someone* is God, and that *something* is heaven. The most important decision you can make is to pursue God and his life. As you intentionally do this, the quality of your life will be elevated, your soul will be refreshed, and you will be surprised at how alive you feel—because you'll find the yearnings of your soul met in the God who loves you more than anything else in the world.

afterword

I've filleted thousands of fish in my lifetime with little more than small nicks and cuts from the filet knife. Maybe I was overdue for a large gash and perhaps I'd become a bit cavalier. But as we slowly trolled back to the harbor, I pulled the beautiful 25 pound King Salmon from the fish box and slapped that bad boy on top of the cooler. My knife, long and sharp, went to work by first slicing around the gills. But the fish was too big for the cooler top, began sliding off, and instinctively I tried catching the fish with my right hand—forgetting that I was holding a knife. Quicker than you can say "Oh fish!" the blade cut across the top of my left hand resulting in a deep four inch gash and lots of blood.

My partner came up with a first aid kit and with a tightly wrapped compress around my hand I was off to the hospital. 17 stitches later I was out of the ER knowing that one inch separated me from a slit wrist and reconstructive surgery. There is always something to be thankful for even while your hand is throbbing with pain—and something to be learned. As my dear mother said, "So next time you catch a big fish, revel in the experience and try to enjoy the boat ride back to shore. Filleting the fish can wait!"

Great advice. There was no reason to have that fished cleaned before hitting the dock. Living life to the full does not mean living life in haste. So, as a final prayer for you, I pray you will learn (along with me) to *revel* more, squeezing the most out of every cruise back to the harbor. Remember that some tasks can wait, while other things cannot—like living in the moment each day of your life. And to that end—CHEERS!

about the author

John Merritt is the Founding Pastor of an influential faith community in San Francisco's East Bay called CrossWinds Church. He serves as consultant, coach and speaker for a network of pastors and churches in the San Francisco Bay Area and across the U.S. John has been called "a pastor trapped in an adventurer's body" because when not behind a pulpit you'll find him lobster diving, helicopter skiing, hauling in yellow fin tuna, or rocketing over whitewater in the Grand Canyon—and that's just a short list. He'd love to hear about your latest adventure at:

pastorjohnmerritt.com

john@pastorjohnmerritt.com

By logging on to John's website, you will find his latest blogs, and will be able to connect with him via Facebook, Twitter and Google+.

CPSIA information can be obtained
at www.ICGtesting.com
Printed in the USA
FSOW02n1218091015
11992FS